100 PROVEN WAYS TO TRANSFORM YOUR COMMUNITY

Other books about the Faithworks movement include:

Faithworks
Faithworks: Stories of Hope
Faithworks: Intimacy & Involvement
Faithworks Unpacked

100 Proven Ways to Transform Your Community

STEVE CHALKE
WITH
ANTHONY WATKIS

EASTBOURNE

ISBN 1 84291 119 8

Published by
KINGSWAY COMMUNICATIONS LTD
Lottbridge Drove, Eastbourne, BN23 6NT, England.
Email: books@kingsway.co.uk

Book design and production for the publishers by
Bookprint Creative Services, P.O. Box 827, BN21 3YJ, England.
Printed in Great Britain.

Contents

Youth

Family

Counselling, Mentoring

7

Hackney Marsh Partnership & Bromley by Bow Centre

Town Planning

Acknowledgements

A book which features 100 projects will necessarily generate a considerable list of people to thank. While we can't name them all here, our heartfelt thanks go to all of those people who have supplied us with information about their projects – we have simply described their excellent work to transform communities, without which this book would not have been written.

We would also like to thank Simon Johnston for firm foundations and helpful conclusions; Chloe Stirling-Smith for enthusiastic support and help with the arduous task of indexing; Peter Brierley for constant encouragement; Aredi Pitsiaeli for patience beyond measure and support on the bad days as well as the good; and the rest of the Faithworks team.

Foreword

We live in an age where it seems that less of the world has more of the world's riches, and more of the world has less and less. Among those who have the most in every way are professed Christians. Yet it has been a deep sadness that so many of us have espoused a gospel which, for some reason, has avoided practical involvement with the poor of this world. In our zeal to share the good news that we are loved simply by the grace of God we have been nervous of that so-called 'epistle of straw'.

> Faith by itself, if it is not accompanied by action, is dead. But someone will say, 'You have faith; I have deeds.' Show me your faith without deeds, and I will show you my faith by what I do. (James 2:17,18)

Nothing excites me more than to learn that there are some of Jesus' friends who are touching the lives of the poor in practical and spiritual ways. Nothing excites me more than to know that as well as sending money to the poor far away, some of Jesus' friends are beginning to touch their own neighbours in their own community, now.

Steve Chalke has a passion to see this come about in every Christian community and has imparted his passion along with training to many congregations. Here are recorded some of the ways God's heart has touched the poor and needy through Christians who tried.

I recommend these ideas to you and hope that having read

them you may touch the lives of those around you in practical and miraculous ways even before a project is born.

Jackie Pullinger, MBE

Introduction

The task of the church is simply to reflect God and in so doing demonstrate a faith that works. I believe that it is through our actions that our faith speaks and we reflect God faithfully. Rather than primarily talking about God we, the church, should be demonstrating God. Demonstrations are hard to ignore. That's why airlines do those safety demonstrations even though the same information is written on cards in the seat pockets.

Jesus once said that he only did what he saw his Father doing. We as the church fulfil the same role as Jesus did when he was on earth, we mediate God to his creation – we are God's representatives on earth. What, then, should we be doing?

The whole story of the Bible boils down to one central fact: God loves people. As Christians our lives should clearly show that same truth. There is simply no getting around it – we should love people; it's our job and our duty, but even more than that it's worship. When we love people we (as God's representatives) are showing them that God loves them, and in faithfully fulfilling our role we are showing God that we love him. The two go together and cannot be split up; faith and works are two sides of the same coin.

But what does it mean to love people? The truth is that it's difficult for us to talk about love without getting ourselves bogged down in the kind of 'hearts and flowers' romanticism with which we are constantly bombarded by the media. However, love is not some ethereal feeling of affection; it has to be seen in action – as they say, 'seeing is believing'. To someone who is starving the words 'God loves you' are meaningless – a square meal, however, might mean the difference between life and death. John Lennon put it succinctly when he sang 'Love is real, real is love.'

Jesus did not want to be crucified. In the garden of Gethsemane he pleaded with his Father for another option. Ultimately, however, he said 'Yet not my will, but yours be done' (Luke 22:42) and his obedient action became the greatest demonstration of the Father's love for us. 'This is how we know what love is: Jesus Christ laid down his life for us' (1 John 3:16). Actions are more powerful than words.

Practically this means that we as a church have got to get our hands dirty. We have to sacrifice time and money and effort to be lovers of people. Unless we do we can't claim to be lovers of God. It's not easy, but then if it were easy it would not be radical, and if it were not radical it wouldn't change the world.

The trouble is that the world has so many problems, so many people in need, that it is difficult to know where to start. That's why I have written this book. I want to encourage you to see that we can make a difference. There are practical ways in which we can show God's love to people around us. But more than that, I want to encourage you to do it. It might be that your church already operates some projects like those featured in this book, or you might currently be looking for a project to start up. Either way I'm sure there is something here to inspire you.

The 100 projects written about in these pages are all different and challenging initiatives. And, more importantly, they are all real and happening – they are not just ideas, they are working models. Each of the projects is complete with contact details (names, addresses, phone numbers, email) so that you can get in touch with them and ask for advice, ask questions, or maybe arrange to visit.

Some of the projects in this book are very big, complex schemes working with hundreds of people and annual budgets of literally millions of pounds. Others are smaller, simpler, and some require little more than time spent showing people love over a cup of coffee. They all have two things in common: they offer hope of transformation to the people they serve and they are constantly developing, because to stand still is to die. It's easy to get discouraged if we focus on the large, obviously successful projects – but that is a mistake; we should be focusing on the people we need to help. Even the tallest trees grow from a small seed. When I started Oasis we just had one project with a couple of staff and a whole load of people who needed to see God's love in action. It's obvious to say that Rome wasn't built in a day, but it's obvious because it's true. We all have to start somewhere – what's important is that we start. I guarantee that there is at least one project in this book that your church could copy in your community, reflecting God and demonstrating that faith works.

Steve Chalke, Founder of Oasis Trust

How to Use this Book

Essentially this book is a directory of ideas, and, much like any other directory, it might not be the kind of book that you would read in a couple of sittings. However, every one of the projects presented in these pages has something different and valuable to offer – your time would not be wasted in reading them all.

The projects in this book address a wide range of needs; they also cover the full spectrum of scale. Some of the items featured would be easy to set up in almost any church, however limited the available resources; others would require significant funding, time and expertise. We have chosen not to classify the projects by their difficulty, however, as even the most elaborate initiative might spark a simple idea that your church could pursue.

Clearly not all of the projects will be suitable for all churches – it depends on what the issues are around you and where you are on the journey! But what might be inappropriate at the moment may be exactly what you need in a few years' time.

The greatest consideration in setting up a project must be the needs of the community it aims to serve. To this end, we recommend that you use this book in conjunction with the Faithworks tools available from our website (www.faithworks.info). The Community Audit will help you to identify the needs of your area, while our Church Audit will enable you to assess the strengths of your church. For more information on these tools see 'How to Get Involved'. We also recommend that you consult *Faithworks Unpacked* which deals with the various practical challenges of starting projects like those featured in this book and offers you a step-by-step guide to turning your ideas into sustainable reality.

So enjoy. Allow these ideas to inspire you – steal them, copy them, change them, combine them, and let them transform your community.

SECTION 1:

Health, Drugs, Prostitution

1. Reigate and Redhill YMCA – Fit for Life

Fit for Life is designed for adults aged 16–90; in fact anyone who is rehabilitating from illness, or who has a disability. It aims to encourage a healthy lifestyle through effective and safe exercise in a friendly environment. Fit for Life serves the residents of Reigate and surrounding areas at a purpose-built sports and leisure centre.

HOW IT WORKS

Fit for Life's clients include people living with physical or sensory impairment, mental health problems and learning disabilities, as well as those rehabilitating from stroke, coronary heart disease or living with Multiple Sclerosis. The project provides top quality service and, in addition to gym facilities, offers specialist activities and classes to people with particular needs, as well as giving advice on the suitability of other public courses to clients with disabilities. Anyone can be accepted onto Fit For Life if they are referred by their doctor, social worker or physiotherapist. People can also refer themselves and may be accepted after an initial medical assessment.

DEVELOPMENT

Fit for Life is always looking for ways to expand its service by inviting groups with specific needs to contact them.

THINGS TO CONSIDER

- What facilities are there in your area for people, young and old, with special needs?
- Does your church have the space needed to start up a gym similar to Fit for Life?

HOW TO GET FUNDING

The YMCA gym was expanded and re-equipped to meet the needs of disabled people. It was funded by Sport England, as well as generous grants from a local foundation and businessman.

FOR ADVICE AND MORE INFORMATION CONTACT:

Penny Stevens,
Fit for Life,
Reigate and Redhill YMCA,
Prince's Road,
Redhill,
Surrey,
RH1 6JJ
Tel: 01737 779979
Fax: 01737 780356

'I think I can safely say that my colleagues and I have benefited from our experiences as much as we have helped our Fit for Life members. Something about the opportunity to connect with each other's humanity.'

2. Maybridge – Handshake Befriending Scheme

Handshake is an activity-based befriending scheme providing voluntary befrienders for people with mental health problems. Initial conversations with local health professionals confirmed a need for low-level support for those patients whose problems are not severe enough to access the psychiatric services. Professional health workers recommend the scheme to suitable patients.

HOW IT WORKS

National research has shown that an overriding need of people with mental health problems is simply to have a friend – a need met by Handshake. The scheme aims to promote mental well-being and independence, with volunteers working to build self-esteem through acceptance, encouragement, value and care. Handshake provides the opportunity for users to enjoy every-day activities and have something to look forward to. As the promotion of independence is a stated goal of the scheme, volunteers operate on a short-term basis to prevent dependency.

DEVELOPMENT

Handshake proposes to establish a system of referrals which will allow them to pass on their users to psychiatric services if their mental health deteriorates over the course of the scheme. A further plan is to develop a drop-in facility for users of the scheme and their families.

THINGS TO CONSIDER

- What is the level of mental health need in your area?
- What professionals can you consult with?

- What professional support or training will staff or volunteers need?
- What referral systems do you need to establish?

HOW TO GET FUNDING

The Nationwide Foundation trust provided Handshake with a grant. West Sussex Community Partnership awarded another small grant from their 'community chest'.

FOR ADVICE AND MORE INFORMATION CONTACT:

The MILE Project,
c/o Maybridge Community Church,
The Strand,
Maybridge,
Worthing,
West Sussex,
BN12 6DL
Tel: 01903 603337
Email: info@mile-project.org.uk
Web: www.mile-project.org.uk

'This is exactly the kind of project we have been needing for years. I can think of lots of people who could benefit from this. I'm sure the scheme will be well used.'

3. Yeldall Manor

Yeldall Manor is a Christian drug and alcohol residential rehabilitation centre which has helped hundreds of people break free of their addictions since it opened in 1977. The Manor is able to house 32 men aged between approximately 20 and 40 on its 46-week programme. The Manor accepts referrals from all over the UK.

HOW IT WORKS

The aim of Yeldall Manor is to free its residents from addictions to drugs and alcohol. To this end Yeldall is a completely drug- and alcohol-free zone and encourages its clients to go through the detoxification process before taking up residency. The Yeldall programme aims to tackle the problems that lead to drug and alcohol dependency rather than just breaking the symptoms. Clients are encouraged to find a purpose in life, a sense of self-worth and to restore broken relationships. Yeldall Manor is committed to families and will do everything possible to support and help close family members of residents, employing a family support worker to undertake this work.

DEVELOPMENT

Yeldall Manor has received funding from the European Social Fund to allow the development of its resettlement programme. This has provided two resettlement workers who assist residents in their ongoing reintegration into society.

THINGS TO CONSIDER

- What services are available for those suffering from addiction in your area?
- How could your church help with this problem?

- What specialist skills and facilities would you need to set up a project like Yeldall Manor?

HOW TO GET FUNDING

The principal source of funding for the Manor is the residents' fees, which are generally provided by their Local Authority or by the Probation Service under Drug Treatment and Testing Orders. Additional funding has come from the European Social Fund, the Learning Skills Council and through the continuing support of individuals, churches and charitable trusts.

FOR ADVICE AND MORE INFORMATION CONTACT:

Yeldall Christian Centres,
Yeldall Manor,
Hare Hatch,
Reading,
Berkshire,
RG10 9XR
Tel: 0118 940 1093
Fax: 0118 940 4852
Email: yeldall@aol.com

'I spent 15 years on drugs and, to cut a long story short, I was in a mess and had been for years. I needed help and got it. I found Yeldall Manor and it saved my life. Through hard work and the will to change, this eleven-month programme works.'

4. Off the Fence – Project Magdalene

During its work with the homeless of Brighton, Off the Fence identified a need to help young, vulnerable, girls and women who are caught in a web of drugs and housing problems and who see their only answer as turning to prostitution.

HOW IT WORKS

Following the example of other agencies, Project Magdalene advertised a drop-in centre and helpline in the hope of reaching and counselling the girls. It was soon discovered, however, that the project would differ from other projects in this area of work. Rather than meeting large numbers of girls who come and go, Project Magdalene has found it has a few clients with whom it develops intensive relationships. The girls do not identify themselves as prostitutes, but rather as drug addicts who support their habit through prostitution. The project aims simply to get alongside these girls and help to free them from their damaging lifestyle.

DEVELOPMENT

Project Magdalene is in its infancy and has big plans for development. It is hoped that funding will become available to open a safe house for women, with a café area to chat, a laundry, showers, a store of clothes and toiletries, and facilities to offer training, education and addiction counselling.

THINGS TO CONSIDER

- Is prostitution an issue in your area? Remember that even if you don't see it, it may still be there.
- How would you go about gaining the trust of an ostracised group?

- What facilities, if any, would you need?
- Could you commit to long-term work, even if it may appear fruitless at first?

HOW TO GET FUNDING

Project Magdalene is funded by local churches and individuals, albeit on a limited scale. Increasingly funding has been sought from charitable organisations, grant-making trusts and secular companies.

FOR ADVICE AND MORE INFORMATION CONTACT:

Off the Fence,
P.O. Box 2206,
Hove,
BN3 8LY
Tel: 01273 733732
Email: info@offthefence.org
Web: www.offthefence.org.uk

'We are determined that in the name of Jesus and by the power of the Holy Spirit we might provide opportunities for all people groups to accept or reject God's invitation to eternal life. Apart from the "mainstream" community this means working with the homeless, the drug addict, the young runaway, the abused, the AIDS sufferer, the prostitute and many more.'

5. Gold Hill Baptist Church – BeFrienders

BeFrienders is a scheme operated by Gold Hill Baptist Church as part of its community and family initiative. The project links volunteers with those in the community who are in need of help or friendship and time invested in them. The trained volunteers meet and befriend the person to whom they are assigned either as a short-term measure or for a longer period.

HOW IT WORKS

The aims of the Gold Hill community and family initiative are to offer a professional service in partnership with other organisations, and to meet the needs of families and individuals in the local community, offering a Christian response to those needs. For the BeFrienders project, this means providing support and friendship, encouragement and practical help to families or individuals within the local community. Contacts are gained through referrals made by health visitors, doctors, Social Services or by direct contact with the community and family worker.

DEVELOPMENT

The long-term vision for the BeFrienders scheme is that every postcode in the UK would have a church operating the project. It is felt that the needs addressed by BeFrienders are universal – were the project emulated in every town in the country, loneliness and isolation would be greatly reduced across the board.

THINGS TO CONSIDER

- What are the needs of your community?
- What could your project do to help meet these needs?
- How can you assess the usefulness of your project? How do

you know that you are achieving what you set out to achieve?

- Could you work in partnership with Gold Hill Baptist Church as it seeks to extend the BeFrienders project?

HOW TO GET FUNDING

The BeFrienders project is funded as part of the Community and Family Initiative. Money is received from individuals who pledge long-term support, cash donations from charitable trusts, and sponsorship from local businesses including Barclays Bank and the Lloyds TSB Foundation.

FOR ADVICE AND MORE INFORMATION CONTACT:

Corinne Jeffery,
Community and Family Worker,
Gold Hill Baptist Church,
Gold Hill Common East,
Chalfont St Peter,
Bucks,
SL9 9DG
Tel: 01753 887173
Email: corinne.jeffery@goldhill.org

'The secular bodies dealing with situations of personal crisis are overburdened. There is a real need for Christians to take up the challenge and demonstrate that we care.'

6. The Lighthouse Project, Hull

Operating from a refitted bus on the streets of Kingston-upon-Hull, the Lighthouse Project reaches out to women working in prostitution. Offering friendship, warm drinks, condoms and, when requested, prayer, the team of staff and volunteers have slowly built up relationships of trust with the women they serve. The bus has a comfy seating area, kitchen and counselling room.

HOW IT WORKS

The Lighthouse Project aims to help women free themselves from prostitution. Although many women would like to escape this lifestyle, they are often deeply in debt, in trouble with the law, living in inadequate and sometimes appalling conditions, and many of them have no education or training. Past histories of abuse and neglect have caused many to turn to heroin. The addiction can seem insurmountable without long-term, one-to-one support. This support is offered by outreach workers who visit the women in their homes, take them to appointments and give them practical help to change their lives. The project has helped about 150 women since it started in 1996.

DEVELOPMENT

The Lighthouse Project eventually hopes to open a safe house, a daytime drop-in centre and a small business which would offer job opportunities to women who have left prostitution.

THINGS TO CONSIDER

- Is prostitution a problem in your area?
- What measures would help the women involved and alleviate the problem?

- What facilities could your church offer to women in prostitution?
- Could you commit to long-term work?

HOW TO GET FUNDING

The Lighthouse Project receives funding from a variety of sources, mainly local and national charitable trusts. A Community Pioneering Award was received from the city of Hull in 2000, helping to raise the profile of the project.

FOR ADVICE AND MORE INFORMATION CONTACT:

The Hull Lighthouse Project,
65 Cottingham Road,
Hull,
HU5 2PP
Tel: 01482 442953
Email: lighthouse@2000k.com

'It's a very, very lonely, evil life . . . it just destroys you, you lose everything through it.'

7. Maybridge – Kickstart

Kickstart is a breakfast club that runs from the local middle school to provide a healthy start to the day and to encourage children to take care of personal health. The school is responsible for identifying pupils for Kickstart by targeting children and families that are in need of the extra support provided by the club.

HOW IT WORKS

Kickstart aims to provide a calm and healthy start to the day for 8–12-year-olds who need a healthy breakfast that they might not get at home. The service has an educational quality promoting healthy living through nutrition, hygiene and oral health. Furthermore, Kickstart offers social and educational support to its members by providing positive mentoring. Through befriending and building up a rapport between staff and students as well as between the pupils themselves, the children's self-esteem is raised. Staff report that pupils are far more responsive in the classroom following a positive start to the day.

DEVELOPMENT

Plans for future development are in the realm of scale. It is hoped that it will be possible to replicate the project in other local schools as well as increasing the number of pupils referred to the existing project. In order to accomplish these goals a full-time Kickstart manager will be appointed.

THINGS TO CONSIDER

- Would your local primary, junior, or secondary school be interested in working with you to provide a breakfast club scheme?

- Do you have a team of volunteers who would commit to getting up early?
- What professional workers do you need to make contact with to promote a health message (i.e. oral health)?
- What training will volunteers need (i.e. basic food hygiene, child protection)?

HOW TO GET FUNDING

Maybridge Community Church provides the salary of the part-time project manager. Other funding is generated by the West Sussex Health Authority healthy living fund and West Sussex Social Services small grants fund.

FOR ADVICE AND MORE INFORMATION CONTACT:

The MILE Project,
c/o Maybridge Community Church,
The Strand,
Maybridge,
Worthing,
West Sussex,
BN12 6DL
Tel: 01903 603337
Email: info@mile-project.org.uk
Web: www.mile-project.org.uk

'Can we have breakfast club every day, and can we have a lunch club and an after dinner club as well?'

8. Trust

Trust is a church and community based project that grew out of local concern for street-working women in Lambeth. It aims to support women involved in prostitution and young women exploited through prostitution. It looks to complement, work alongside and refer to existing services. Trust offers friendship and support in a confidential, safe and non-judgemental environment.

HOW IT WORKS

Trust is currently responsible for three weekly street outreaches in Streatham and Brixton, which provide hot drinks and chocolate. These allow relationships to be built with the women and enable the Trust workers to offer them help and support. The women are given a contact card and invited to the Trust Drop-In, at which they can simply relax and have some time away from the streets. They also have access to help and support around a number of issues such as accommodation, drug and alcohol treatment, counselling, health and legal issues. The women can have a shower, cook meals, get clothing, wash their clothes and have a locker.

DEVELOPMENT

Trust's plans for the future include strengthening links with the local church, developing a 'Court Diversion' scheme within the Criminal Justice system, and the establishment of a schools programme to promote healthy relationships.

THINGS TO CONSIDER

- Is prostitution a problem in your area?
- How might your church work towards helping women

involved in prostitution and other groups on the fringe of society?

- What facilities would you need to realise your goals?
- Could you work in partnership with churches or other groups already working with women involved in prostitution?

HOW TO GET FUNDING

Trust has been funded by donations and is now in the process of bidding for local authority funding as well as making applications to trust and grant-making bodies.

FOR ADVICE AND MORE INFORMATION CONTACT:

Diane Martin,
Trust,
St Mark's Centre,
London,
SW11 1EJ
Tel: 0794 6334271
Email: trustdi@ukonline.co.uk

'We want to continue to communicate through our actions that the women we work with are not forgotten, but are unique and valuable people who are made in the image of God.'

SECTION 2:

Homelessness

9. Spires

Spires is a full-time facility serving South London's homeless population. The centre's first point of contact has remained largely constant within its twelve-year life: the distribution of food and clothes to those who need them. However, over time it has developed beyond this basic service and now offers training, health facilities, legal advice and drug/alcohol rehabilitation.

HOW IT WORKS

Spires' ultimate goal is to house those who sleep rough as well as the unrecognised homeless – those who stay in hostels, bed and breakfasts or on friends' floors. The centre recognises that permanently housing people is only possible if they have the necessary skills to maintain themselves once resettled. To this end, the centre offers its clients a seven-week 'life skills' training course. This focuses on such areas as budgeting, nutrition, practical household skills and first aid. Other courses are available in IT and literacy and numeracy. These training opportunities help the centre's clients to find employment and housing and lead to their reintegration into society.

DEVELOPMENT

In the future it is hoped that the centre will offer accredited training such as NVQs. It also plans to establish partnerships with local agencies to allow its clients to undertake placements as volunteers.

THINGS TO CONSIDER

- Is homelessness a problem in your area?
- Are other organisations meeting the needs of the community?

- Do you have the resources to set up this kind of project?
  — time and talent
  — buildings
  — finance
- How could you access the resources you do not have currently?

HOW TO GET FUNDING

Spires is funded by grant-making trusts, churches, schools, local companies, charity shops and voluntary sources such as fundraising events. It has also received funding from the Community Fund (previously known as the National Lottery Charities Board).

FOR ADVICE AND MORE INFORMATION CONTACT:

Frances Newell,
8 Tooting Bec Gardens,
London,
SW16 1RB
Tel: 0208 696 0943
Fax: 0208 696 9627
Email: spires@hostels.org.uk

'I was wrecking my life through drink – sleeping in the church-yard and in really bad health. I finally managed to break the habit after Spires got me into detox. Now I have a job, a flat and I'm married with a small baby!'

10. The Oasis Health Centre

The Oasis Health Centre is a drop-in primary health centre for homeless and vulnerable people, providing showers and washing facilities, a nurse, hairdresser, clothing, laundry service, chiropodist, dentist, benefits advice and advocacy. It sees 65–75 clients per day, giving 30–40 showers and taking in 40 bags of washing.

HOW IT WORKS

The Oasis Health Centre affords its visitors the dignity of basic services that we all take for granted. Minor injuries can be treated, without the need to wait for hours in A & E, with time and care being invested in the person. With volunteers working alongside full-time staff, relationships are fostered with clients. Health advice is given aiming to promote good health among the homeless and insecurely housed – prevention being better than cure.

DEVELOPMENT

Current areas of development include the advocacy function of the Health Centre. This is being accomplished through a more proactive approach to helping people rebuild their lives, involving links with detoxification and rehabilitation centres, as well as working with people one to one to encourage them while they are still using the centre's services.

THINGS TO CONSIDER

- What facilities are open to the homeless in your area?
- Do you have premises that have facilities which the homeless could use? These might include:
    — showers

— laundry
— kitchen
● What specialist services could you offer?

HOW TO GET FUNDING

The Oasis Health Centre receives no government funding. Trusts, churches and individual supporters meet its running costs of £160,000 per annum.

FOR ADVICE AND MORE INFORMATION CONTACT:

Daniel Wheeler,
Tel: 020 7401 9684
Fax: 020 7771 0755
Email: ohc@oasistrust.org

Or write to:
Maureen Erny,
The Oasis Centre,
115 Southwark Bridge Road,
London,
SE1 0AX

'The Oasis Health Centre provides a haven for those who have no one else they can trust and nowhere else they can feel safe. Staff at the centre build up some great relationships with people using the facilities, and it's amazing to see lives changed as a result.'

11. Caring Hands in the Community

Caring Hands is a Christian charity that has been working with the homeless of Medway for some years, during which time it has identified many needs within its community. A comprehensive range of services is provided to help meet these needs. The centre offers food, showers, hairdressing, a clothing and laundry service and much more.

HOW IT WORKS

The centre plays host to two local GPs who conduct a surgery for the homeless, rough sleepers and others who do not have access to a GP. Caring Hands also helps to find housing for the homeless people it meets, referring them to various hostels, landlords and housing associations with whom it has established a relationship over the years. Other services offered are open to the wider community, including a drug and alcohol information clinic run in partnership with Social Services, literacy classes for adults who are unable to read, a legal advice service and pregnancy crisis advice. On top of this the centre also provides a furniture project, internet access and computer training.

DEVELOPMENT

Caring Hands aims to offer an increasingly holistic service. A planned 24-hour hostel will enable greater involvement with many of its clients.

THINGS TO CONSIDER

- What areas of need can you identify in your community?
- What methods of research can you use to confirm that these needs exist?

- How might your church work to meet these needs?
- Of all the initiatives run by Caring Hands, which could your church emulate?

HOW TO GET FUNDING

Caring Hands is almost exclusively funded by the local church – an amazing fact considering its scale. However, in recent months there have been some encouraging moves from national funding agencies expressing an interest. The local council are also keen to see where they may have available resources for funding.

FOR ADVICE AND MORE INFORMATION CONTACT:

Caring Hands in the Community,
Bridge House,
New Road Avenue,
Chatham,
Kent,
ME4 6BA
Tel: 01634 409768

'Caring Hands has fast become a sanctuary for the needy and homeless of Medway and beyond. The non-judgemental approach of the staff helps in reaching folk who for the most part have simply made some wrong decisions in life.'

12. Yeldall Homeless Projects

Yeldall Homeless Projects, in partnership with Shaftesbury Housing Association, offer a unique style of supported accommodation to young homeless people in the London Boroughs of Hillingdon and Hounslow. The Yeldall projects provide both hostels (a total of 21 beds) and a programme of education and training called 'Streetworks'.

HOW IT WORKS

Yeldall recognises that for many young people, homelessness is a symptom of deeper alienation. As the structure of community becomes more fragile, many young people are deprived of models for living. Those who are made homeless in the formative stages of their adulthood feel this most acutely. Yeldall sees that there is little point in providing a roof over someone's head if they have no inner foundation for life, and hopes to help its residents take stock of their lives and regain their self-esteem and confidence. Streetworks aims to build confidence as well as life and employment skills through basic literacy and numeracy training, help with CVs, interviews and job search.

DEVELOPMENT

As part of their ongoing development, Yeldall Homeless Projects have launched a café and charity shop, providing fundraising and community building opportunities.

THINGS TO CONSIDER

- Is homelessness a significant problem in your area?
- In what ways could your church start to tackle this problem?
- What facilities would you need to open a hostel for the homeless?

HOW TO GET FUNDING

The two arms of Yeldall's homeless work are funded independently. The hostel accommodation costs are met by housing benefit and some funding from Supporting People – Section 106. (Visit www.spkweb.org.uk). Streetworks has been funded by a variety of sources and is currently applying for funds from the European Social Fund, the Single Regeneration Budget, the Association for London Government and the Learning Skills Council.

FOR ADVICE AND MORE INFORMATION CONTACT:

Yeldall Homeless Projects,
Barnhill Methodist Church,
Welbeck Avenue,
Hayes,
Middlesex,
UB4 9EZ
Tel: 020 8797 9500
Fax: 020 8797 9666
Email: homeless@yeldall.org.uk

'My six-month training period ends at Christmas, so I'm currently applying for new jobs, including a job at a solicitor's, with a possibility of becoming a legal secretary, something I would never have considered before coming to Yeldall. I am much more confident, and feel that I can do anything now.'

13. Oasis Housing @ No. 3

No. 3 is a hostel for young homeless females aged between 16–25. Initially residents are provided with an all-inclusive service package including food, electricity and laundry tokens. After six months they move into the second stage of the accommodation where they live more independently in preparation for life beyond No. 3.

HOW IT WORKS

Through the learning experience of their first six months living in community, cooking for each other and receiving the support of a family environment, the girls are able to make a move towards independence. Each resident is assigned a case-worker who not only supports and counsels them, but will eventually help them through the process of moving from the hostel into stable accommodation and employment – the ultimate aim of the project. Efforts are made to find permanent accommodation for the residents in partnership with Southwark Council. The support and training they have received enables the girls to live independently and not become homeless again, freeing them from the cycle of homelessness.

DEVELOPMENT

A peer education project is being developed in which the girls go out to schools and youth groups and talk on issues such as homelessness, working alongside Oasis staff from other projects.

THINGS TO CONSIDER

- Is homelessness a problem in your area?
- Is any other agency offering a service like No. 3, with which you could be involved?
- Do you have the financial wherewithal to set up a project which requires both buildings and full-time, live-in, staff?
- Could you work with other churches to set up a project like No. 3?

HOW TO GET FUNDING

Oasis Housing @ No. 3 costs approximately £160,000 per annum to run: 75% of this is provided through statutory funding, the balance through trusts and supporters.

FOR ADVICE AND MORE INFORMATION CONTACT:

Abbe Stapleton,
Tel: 020 7639 5505
Email: oasishousing@no3.org.uk

Or write to:
Maureen Erny,
The Oasis Centre,
115 Southwark Bridge Road,
London,
SE1 0AX

'Oasis Housing @ No.3 is a unique place and it is a pleasure to work here. The residents and staff, current and past, have all contributed to making No. 3 a home, not just a hostel.'

14. Oasis – The Foyer @ Croydon

A Foyer offers safe, affordable accommodation to vulnerable and homeless young people. Additionally it provides training, educational and employment opportunities to both its residents and the wider community. There are 114 Foyers operating in the UK. Since it opened in June 2000, the Foyer @ Croydon has been home to 40 young people.

HOW IT WORKS

The Foyer @ Croydon aims to integrate its 18 young people into the community. This is accomplished through training to help residents find employment, assistance in finding stable accommodation, and life skills training in order to avoid future homelessness. Soon clients who complete these courses will be awarded an accredited certificate in recognition of their achievement. The Foyer @ Croydon is now fully accredited by the Foyer Federation.

DEVELOPMENT

The new IT suite and internet café will offer cyberskills training at various levels to both Foyer tenants and socially excluded people within the local community.

THINGS TO CONSIDER

- Does the Foyer Federation already operate a project in your area?
- If not, is there a need for such a project in your area? What research can you carry out to assess this?
- Having identified a need, what practical solutions can you plan? *Faithworks Unpacked* contains full details of research and planning techniques.

HOW TO GET FUNDING

The Foyer @ Croydon is a partnership project. The Foyer building is owned by Broomleigh Housing Association and was partly funded by Croydon Council. Young people in Croydon churches raised around £100,000 to help get the project started. Oasis Trust is the Managing Agent. Ongoing costs will be met by Supporting People, Single Regeneration Budget funding as well as through various trusts.

FOR ADVICE AND MORE INFORMATION CONTACT:

Ebi Ajuka,
Tel: 020 8239 6066
Email: foyer@oasistrust.org

Or write to:
Maureen Erny,
The Oasis Centre,
115 Southwark Bridge Road,
London,
SE1 0AX

'The Foyer is a very positive environment. It's not just about having a place to stay. It's about preparing young people for the future. It's amazing to see the transformation in a young person once they realise we are here for them and want to equip them to face the future with confidence.'

15. Bethany Christian Trust

Bethany Christian Trust was set up in 1983 in response to steadily increasing numbers of homeless people in the city of Edinburgh. The initial goal of the trust was to provide hostel accommodation for homeless people and also to address the underlying causes of their situation. From this vision the trust has grown beyond all measure.

HOW IT WORKS

The original hostel operated by the trust was outgrown and so an adjacent derelict building was bought and converted. From this base the trust was able to extend the service it offered to include a supported accommodation department for people with special needs and addictions. The Trust now aims to support people from the street right through the process of reintegrating them into society. Its goal is to empower the homeless to achieve their potential. To do this it operates a van which meets the immediate needs of rough sleepers, emergency accommodation, structured resettlement programmes, and medium- to long-term tenancies. It currently employs 79 staff and has an annual budget of £2 million.

DEVELOPMENT

Along with other agencies, Bethany has had a tremendous impact on the homelessness problem of Edinburgh. However, it recognises that there is still much to do. It continues to strive to eradicate the problem.

THINGS TO CONSIDER

- Is homelessness a problem in your area?
- What steps could your church make to become part of

the solution?

- What facilities and expertise do you have?
- How might you obtain further facilities and professional input?
- Could you work in partnership with other churches in your area?

HOW TO GET FUNDING

Bethany Christian Trust has been funded by a number of groups. These include local authority funding for rent and support of those with special needs, Scottish Executive grants, money for New Deal placements, etc. Further to this is funding from Christian grant-making trusts, individuals, churches and Bethany's own chain of seven charity shops.

FOR ADVICE AND MORE INFORMATION CONTACT:

Iain Gordon,
Bethany Christian Trust,
18 Jane Street,
Edinburgh,
EH6 5HD
Tel: 0131 467 3030
Email: Iain-Gordon@bethanyct.com
Web: www.bethanychristiantrust.com

To read more about the Bethany Trust, see *Faithworks: Stories of Hope.*

'We believe that it is tremendously important that our faith stays at the heart of Bethany Christian Trust. Our whole ethos is to provide a holistic response to the needs of homeless people in the name of Jesus Christ.'

16. Kingston Terrace

Sister Eileen Carroll has lived in a ground floor flat in a Georgian terrace house near Leeds city centre since 1996; a flat which she opens up to local homeless people who frequently struggle with alcohol abuse. While in her flat, the visitors receive support and training and, more importantly, experience love.

HOW IT WORKS

On Wednesdays and Thursdays Kingston Terrace is open to its regular visitors. Sometimes they bring food for a shared lunch or make a small donation. Their time is spent tidying and improving the garden and communal areas of the flat, as well as producing such items as bird boxes, window boxes and novelty notebooks. These products are made in a cellar workshop and the income derived from their sale is donated to charities. Eileen provides no material handouts to her visitors. Instead her response to their chaotic and broken lives is to give them dignity and a sense of belonging to a local community.

DEVELOPMENT

It is difficult to plan how Kingston Terrace will develop. Essentially Sister Eileen is developing a new form of community work or church.

THINGS TO CONSIDER

- Living and working among those you are trying to serve is not easy. Having the support of your community, church or organisation is essential. It is very easy to become immersed in the work and not take time out for yourself or your family.

Is this something to which you could commit a period of your life?

HOW TO GET FUNDING

Many councils that have social housing in run-down, poor estates have hard to let properties. There are a number of church groups and voluntary organisations that obtain leases on such empty properties on a rent-free basis on the understanding that they will operate a community project from the premises. Contact your local housing department or Council for Voluntary Organisations for more details.

FOR ADVICE AND MORE INFORMATION CONTACT:

Sister Eileen Carroll,
c/o Caritas Social Action,
39 Eccleston Square,
London,
SW1V 1BX
Tel: 020 7901 4875
Web: www.caritas-socialaction.org.uk

'Living on the street is hard; everybody just treats you like dirt and you don't have much hope. It's nice to go somewhere where you know people will treat you like a person . . . and still like you when you screw things up.'

17. Banbury Homes – The Banbury Foyer

Banbury Homes, a Shaftesbury Housing Group project, opened the Banbury Foyer in November 1999. The Foyer exists to provide housing and education to young people from the Cherwell District Council area of North Oxfordshire. The centre can house 19 young people who would otherwise be homeless or living in insecure accommodation.

HOW IT WORKS

Rather than offering 'take it or leave it' services to those it houses, the Banbury Foyer provides housing on the basis of a wider contract. The young people it serves are contractually obliged to attend college, take on training or go out to work. Only if these conditions (and other rules relating to behaviour) are met is their place in the Foyer secure. Ultimately, the Foyer looks to enable its clients to support themselves, offering independent living skills training to accomplish this goal.

DEVELOPMENT

In the future it is hoped that having lived at the Banbury Foyer will be seen as a stamp of quality – an addition to any CV. The goal is that future employers and landlords should think more highly of any young person because they have been through the Foyer.

THINGS TO CONSIDER

- Is there a Foyer currently operating in your area?
- What other housing projects are there available to young people?
- If you were to set up a project like the Banbury Foyer, what difficulties would you expect to face? How might you overcome them?

HOW TO GET FUNDING?

The Banbury Foyer is funded through the Shaftesbury Housing Group. Much of the money needed comes from the Housing Benefit received by clients, which includes Transitional Housing Benefit. A high level of funding is received from Supporting People.

FOR ADVICE AND MORE INFORMATION CONTACT:

Hillary Woods,
The Banbury Foyer,
2 Mawl Court,
58 George Street,
Banbury,
OX16 5BH
Tel: 01295 270075
Email: hcw@banburyhomes.org.uk
Web. www.banburyhomes.org.uk

'Set up to provide accommodation and a fresh start for young homeless people, the Foyer insists that residents agree to undergo some form of education or training. Residents eventually move on to take up their rightful place in society.'

SECTION 3:

Youth

18. Elevate

Inspired by the perennial problems associated with boredom among the youth of the area, Ignite Trust decided to start a dance project: Elevate. With 90 members signed up and an average attendance of 40–50, Elevate provides space to explore dance and to give training and encouragement to young people, in a safe, drug-free environment.

HOW IT WORKS

Elevate is essentially a project that creates a sense of community among its members. In spite of their different backgrounds, firm friendships have been established among the young people. In a supportive environment working towards common goals the members grow in confidence, which affects all areas of their lives including their social and educational development. The group performs at local events, giving an incentive to work hard as well as experience of performance. Some of the young people involved in the project express an interest in Christian faith, and a study group has been set up to meet their needs and answer their questions.

DEVELOPMENT

Originally instructors ran the dance tuition at Elevate. However, as a result of the growing abilities of some of the young people, it is hoped that teaching will increasingly be undertaken by existing members. This will foster even wider skills by giving them experience of teaching and the responsibilities of leadership.

THINGS TO CONSIDER

- What facilities are open to young people in your area?
- Do you have young, energetic people in your church who could invest time and energy in a project like Elevate?
- Do you have access to a suitable venue? If you don't have a hall that could be used, could you use a building operated by your local council?
- What would you identify as the goals of your project? How could you better accomplish these?

HOW TO GET FUNDING

Currently the Elevate project is being funded exclusively by the Ignite church. However, in the long term additional support will be needed as costs grow. To this end, Elevate has approached Harrow Council as well as grant-making trusts for ongoing funding.

FOR ADVICE AND MORE INFORMATION CONTACT:

Elevate,
c/o 268A Kenton Road,
Kenton,
Middlesex,
HA3 8DB
Tel: Cindy (dance project and life skills) 07761 103139
Tel: Dan (DJ workshops, dance and emcee projects) 07949 784122
Email: outreach@ignitetrust.org.uk
Web: www.ignitetrust.org.uk

'Elevate is wicked . . . we love to dance.'

19. Higher Force Challenge

Based in the Shankill Road area of Belfast, Higher Force Challenge is an eight-week course for young people. In an area of high unemployment, crime, drug and alcohol abuse, as well as paramilitary violence, it is easy for young people to be swamped by feelings of hopelessness and to be sucked into the same lifestyle. Higher Force Challenge gives them another choice.

HOW IT WORKS

The Higher Force Challenge programme is designed to help its participants become positive contributors to the life of the Shankill community, rather than part of its problem. The young people enrolled on the course are helped to gain a better understanding of, and respect for, themselves and their community across the sectarian divide. The course explores life issues such as drugs, violence, sectarianism, health and education; the ultimate aim being to teach the young people how to make good choices and take responsibility for their actions. Higher Force Challenge deals with people from both sides of the sectarian divide, offering them a chance to befriend and understand those with whom they have been in conflict. So far more than 300 young people have been through the programme.

DEVELOPMENT

The Higher Force Challenge programme is constantly enrolling new youngsters and working to improve the quality of the service it offers.

THINGS TO CONSIDER

- What issues face the young people in your area?
- Is racial tension a problem that you could address?
- How might you divert young people from a life involved with drugs, drink, violence and crime?

HOW TO GET FUNDING

Higher Force Challenge works in partnership with the probation service who provide much of its funding. Other sources of revenue are the International Fund for Ireland, Smiths Charity, Youth Net, Children in Need and other peace and reconciliation agencies.

FOR ADVICE AND MORE INFORMATION CONTACT:

Jack McKee,
Stadium Youth & Community Projects,
271 Shankill Road,
Belfast,
BT13 1FT
Tel: 01232 223355
Email: newlife@breathemail.net
Web: www.newlifeministriesireland.co.uk/hfc

To read more of the Higher Force Challenge story read *Faithworks: Stories of Hope.*

'My dream is that one day Shankill may be an example to the world of the reconciliation God can bring to a divided area.'

20. JAC

Just Around the Corner (JAC) is a registered youth and community charity working with the young people of Woodley and surrounding areas. It works with schools and existing youth clubs as well as doing outreach work in parks and on the streets.

HOW IT WORKS

Over the last three years, JAC has gained the trust and support of many local young people, helping them to make positive choices by offering them friendship and support as well as providing appropriate education and information on issues relevant to them. Each outreach session has, on average, a team of six volunteers, some of whom are young people who are committed to working with their peers. Volunteers put in the time and effort to get alongside vulnerable young people and support them in making positive choices about their lifestyle and future. JAC wants to see each young person given the opportunity to make something of their life.

DEVELOPMENT

A new exhibition trailer and Mitsubushi Shogun have been purchased which allow JAC to set up anywhere at any time to provide a complete mobile youth club. The trailer has its own sound system, lighting, coffee bar, tables and chairs.

THINGS TO CONSIDER

- How might your church provide innovative solutions to the needs of young people in your area?
- If the kids won't come to your youth club, could you find a way to take your youth club to the kids?

- Could you do this in partnership with other local churches?

HOW TO GET FUNDING

JAC is a non-profit-making charity and the young people have free use of its facilities. JAC receives support and funding from the local churches, Woodley Town Council, Wokingham District Council and other trusts.

FOR ADVICE AND MORE INFORMATION CONTACT:

Sam Milligan,
JAC Outreach,
P.O. Box 4850,
Woodley,
RG5 3XJ
Tel: 0118 441444
Email: info@jacoutreach.org
Web: www.jacoutreach.org

'Our goal is simply this: to give hope to young people in the community, enabling them to make positive choices, by demonstrating love and acceptance according to Christian principles.'

21. Wetherby Young Offenders Institution

An initiative of the YMCA, the Wetherby Young Offenders Institution (WYOI) project aims to befriend sentenced and unsentenced young people in order to develop trusting relationships with them, provide positive role models and facilitate their reintegration into their home communities, thus enabling them to become positive citizens.

HOW IT WORKS

The Wetherby project has, over the last two years, consisted of two main elements. First, a programme of training and education during the young person's stay at the WYOI, which offers Youth Achievement Awards as well as Key Skills courses (Problem Solving, Working with Others, Improving Your Learning and Performance) to trainees on a one-to-one basis around subjects in which they are interested. Second, a programme of ongoing support upon the young person's release, which helps them find the right education and employment opportunities as they rebuild their lives outside of prison.

DEVELOPMENT

Plans for the future include an information/drop-in/youth and homework centre within the prison. Also planned is a scheme to give young offenders a voice in communities outside of prison, and an opportunity to benefit positively the lives of other young people. This will include making music CDs and documentary-style videos.

THINGS TO CONSIDER

- Could your church work with young offenders, encouraging their growth and rehabilitation?

- If it would be impractical to work with a Young Offenders Institution, could your church work with the young people on release?
- What obstacles prevent you from setting up a project like this, and how might you overcome them?

HOW TO GET FUNDING

WYOI is part of YMCA's PIPs (Partnerships in Prisons) project funded by the Prison Service (Youth Justice Board) and part-funded by YMCA England.

FOR ADVICE AND MORE INFORMATION CONTACT:

Steven Fox,
Project Manager,
YMCA Partnerships in Prisons,
HMYOI Wetherby,
York Road,
Wetherby,
LS22 5ED
Tel: 01937 585141 ext. 420
Fax: 01937 583016

'The best thing is when they call you to say thank you because if it had not been for the YMCA they would have never had these new opportunities . . . that is why I do my job.'

22. The WIRE Project – The Crew

The WIRE project (Wick, Information, Recreation and Education) was set up in 1996. Working in partnership with various local organisations the project manager shared a passion to see the regeneration of a run-down estate. The WIRE now runs a wealth of community building activities, employing 20 people with over 200 volunteers, many of whom have been trained for their work.

HOW IT WORKS

One of WIRE's initiatives is The Crew. Inspired by a visit to a local woman's home which was in a state of disrepair and seemed an inadequate environment in which to raise her four children, WIRE project manager Paul Sanderson recognised a need that he could meet. He offered to take her children out once a week to allow her some time for herself. This simple kindness has escalated into a project which picks up 40 children each week. The children benefit from an outing, which broadens their horizons, develops their self-esteem, increases their confidence and introduces them to project workers who become positive role models. The parents benefit from a rest, giving them more energy to invest in their children when they come home.

DEVELOPMENT

The Crew has developed from humble beginnings, a simple idea that could be emulated in any environment across the UK.

THINGS TO CONSIDER

- How would your church go about setting up a project like The Crew?

- What local facilities or attractions could you take children to?
- How would you gain the trust of parents?
- What legal considerations must you make? Remember volunteers must be police-checked.

HOW TO GET FUNDING

Local authorities have small pots of funding for after-school activities. Social services, leisure departments and local councils have funded The Crew as it fulfils the criteria of leisure activities, team-building and creative after-school care.

FOR ADVICE AND MORE INFORMATION CONTACT:

Jon Jolly,
The WIRE project,
Wickbourne Chapel,
Clun Road
Littlehampton,
BN17 7EA
Tel: 01903 731796
Email: jon@thewireproject.com

To read more about the WIRE project, see *Faithworks: Stories of Hope.*

'The staff on The Crew are a dedicated team of trained, police-checked workers both paid and voluntary, who aim to provide new challenges and varied outings for the young people in their care. They each work relationally, making time for the individual as well as the group and aiming to be a small but significant part of their history: both present and future.'

23. Cornerstone Community Project – The Gap

The Cornerstone Church was set up in 1990 in Swansea. Working on an estate of 12,000 houses which suffered greatly from drug abuse, car crime, high youth unemployment and teenage pregnancy rates, the church launched a community project to try to meet the needs of local residents. A building was bought which opened in 1997.

HOW IT WORKS

One of the initiatives run by the Cornerstone Community Project is a development project for disaffected young people called 'The Gap'. The project works with young people who are struggling academically, are from troubled backgrounds, have been in trouble with the police, or are victims of the many other problems which beset local youngsters. The Gap is more than just a youth project for helping troubled kids; it's a system that re-educates, re-motivates and re-engages young people who have been alienated by traditional forms of learning. The primary work of The Gap is with a local girls' school, from which it takes on 15 of the most disruptive pupils each year. The girls are taken through training programmes from the Open College Network for three days a week.

DEVELOPMENT

The Gap is constantly working to develop new partnerships in order to offer greater mentoring opportunities to the young people with whom it works.

THINGS TO CONSIDER

- Could you operate a programme such as The Gap in your community?
- Does your church have teaching staff who could commit to a project such as this?
- How might you establish a relationship with schools to enable you to start a project like The Gap?

HOW TO GET FUNDING

The Cornerstone project receives funding from a number of sources including grant-making trusts. However, the ongoing support of the church members has also been a major source of income.

FOR ADVICE AND MORE INFORMATION CONTACT:

Julian Richards,
Cornerstone Community Project,
32 Mynydd Newydd Road,
Penlan,
Swansea
Tel: 01792 516031
Fax: 01792 516032
Email: julianrichards@cornerstonechurch.co.uk
Web: www.cornerstoneproject.co.uk

To read more about the Cornerstone story, see *Faithworks: Stories of Hope.*

'We've seen some young people become Christians and others hopefully will in the future. But quite besides that, if their experience of Cornerstone has helped to break down their suspicion of the church, then that is a very positive influence in their lives.'

24. Woodley Baptist Church – The Venue

A Woodley Baptist Church initiative, The Venue was born out of the need for a safe place for young people to hang out, be cared for and given life skills that would help them develop into good citizens. Local young people continually asked for a place where they could hang out after school and in the evenings. The Venue provides this.

HOW IT WORKS

The Venue seeks to provide for the needs of young people and, as a result, prove a benefit to the whole community. The Venue is open to all young people in the area and hosts a wide variety of activities. It is housed in a self-contained unit with purpose-built facilities, which include a non-alcoholic bar, internet café, games area and computer games consoles. In addition it serves food. The project is staffed in the main by volunteers, including young people who wish to develop their leadership skills.

DEVELOPMENT

The Venue is viewed as a long-term venture. Plans for the future include a greater emphasis on mentoring and skills training.

THINGS TO CONSIDER

- What facilities are available to the young people in your area?
- Does your church currently run a youth programme? If so, how might you make this more accessible to unchurched young people?
- If your church encourages unchurched young people to

attend its youth programmes, how would you handle problems of drug and alcohol abuse, aggression, etc.?

HOW TO GET FUNDING

The Venue has been funded largely by Woodley Baptist Church. However, much of its equipment has been provided through finance from various organisations and trusts. Additionally some funding has been received from the local council as well as through fundraising by the kids who use the project.

FOR ADVICE AND MORE INFORMATION CONTACT:

James Simmonds,
The Venue,
Woodley Baptist Church,
Hurricane Way,
Woodley,
Reading,
RG5 4UX
Tel: 0118 969 9956
Email: info@woodleyvenue.org.uk
Web: www.woodleyvenue.org.uk

'Young people's lives are being transformed . . . all they want is for you to listen and care.'

25. Perth YMCA Drop-In Centre

Five years ago Perth YMCA borrowed a hall from the local Episcopal church in order to open a drop-in centre for the young people of the area. A group of volunteers was gathered and the centre now opens its doors to around 35 young people every Saturday night. The club's goal is to provide a reliable support network.

HOW IT WORKS

The overall aim of the Perth drop-in centre is to establish relationships with the young people who use it. The teenagers who attend express their primary needs as being somewhere to go, something to do and someone to talk to. Out of the relationships developed with the young people by the club's staff, various other activities have emerged (a football team, day trips, pizza and video evenings, etc.) all of which continue to build positive contacts and offer both entertainment and education opportunities.

DEVELOPMENT

As a result of significant amounts of external funding, the drop-in centre now operates out of its own dedicated premises. It still provides the same basic service but is now in the process of developing a range of exciting new ventures in partnership with other local organisations.

THINGS TO CONSIDER

- What are the needs of the young people in your area?
- What facilities, if any, are there for those young people?
- What facilities does your church have that could be opened up to young people?

- How might you 'get alongside' the young people your project will meet?

HOW TO GET FUNDING

The Perth YMCA Drop-in Centre has received funding from a number of grant-making trusts, such as the Lloyds TSB Foundation for Scotland and Children in Need. This funding has been crucial in the expansion of the existing work and the development of new projects.

FOR ADVICE AND MORE INFORMATION CONTACT:

Ian Marr, Chief Executive,
Perth and District YMCA,
The Y Centre,
19 Atholl Street,
Perth,
PH1 5NH
Tel: 01738 629883
Email: ian@ymcaperth.com
Web: www.ymcaperth.com

'My daughter has developed skills she (and we) never knew she had. She is more likely to try to resolve an argument than to create one now. She is more confident in herself and her abilities.'

26. The WIRE Project – Dance Nation

The WIRE project (Wick, Information, Recreation and Education) was set up in 1996. Working in partnership with various local organisations the project manager shared a passion to see the regeneration of a run-down estate. The WIRE now runs a wealth of community building activities, employing 20 people with over 200 volunteers, many of whom have been trained for their work.

HOW IT WORKS

The Dance Nation project is an after-school dance club for children and young people, which aims to exercise, entertain and educate the young people who attend. Dance Nation employs a dance instructor to teach them the kind of routines they see on *Top of the Pops* and other shows. Halfway through each session is a break time in which the children are given healthy snacks and drinks and education about nutrition, healthy living as well as subjects such as smoking and self-esteem. The project has met with great success and at the end of each summer term puts on a show of its work. The dancers are regularly invited to perform at community events such as local fêtes and the Wick Festival – another WIRE initiative.

DEVELOPMENT

The Dance Nation project developed out of an idea originally raised by community members, and was launched as soon as funding and a suitable instructor was found.

THINGS TO CONSIDER

- Does your church building have a hall suitable for a dance project, or could you hire another venue? Remember that

not all floors are suitable for exercise programmes.
- Do you have people in your church who could:
  - — teach dance to children?
  - — educate children in the breaks?
  - — help out with refreshments?
- Would you charge the children for attending?
- Do you have good partnerships to help promote the project?

HOW TO GET FUNDING

The Dance Nation project received a local council grant to cover its start-up costs for the first two years. This grant pays for the instructor. Further costs are met by support from the local Primary Care Trust and session fees of £1.30 per child, per week (however, in cases where the parents cannot afford this amount, the child may still attend).

FOR ADVICE AND MORE INFORMATION CONTACT:

Heather Sanderson,
The WIRE Project,
Wickbourne Chapel,
Clun Road,
Littlehampton,
BN17 7EA
Email: info@thewireproject.com

To read more about the WIRE project, see *Faithworks: Stories of Hope.*

'We have even been on Saturday morning TV for the programme Live and Kicking, *where our kids met Steps!'*

27. Christ Church Peckham – The Venue

Anyone familiar with the game 'Monopoly' will know that Old Kent Road is not the site of London's most desirable properties. However, this view is not shared by Christ Church Peckham. The church is situated between several large blocks of flats in an area of great need. There would be little for young people to do were it not for The Venue.

HOW IT WORKS

Essentially The Venue is a youth club much like any other (it has the usual pool and table tennis tables, computer games and tuck shop). However, it is extraordinary in two ways. First, for the young people of East Peckham there is literally nothing else to do – were it not for The Venue many of the kids would have to spend their time hanging around on street corners. Second, due to the nature of the area, The Venue attracts kids from a wide variety of ethnic backgrounds. It has become a place in which skin colour is not a barrier to friendship.

DEVELOPMENT

The Venue seeks to offer an increasingly professional service. To this end it plans to refurbish its hall and extend its opening hours.

THINGS TO CONSIDER

- What facilities are available to the young people of your area?
- How might you be able to open up your church buildings to young people?
- Do you have sufficient volunteers to staff a project like The Venue?

- What equipment would you need, how much would it cost, and how would you pay for it?

HOW TO GET FUNDING

The Venue is currently funded entirely by Christ Church, who also provide the hall in which it meets. It is currently in the process of applying for funding from statutory sources.

FOR ADVICE AND MORE INFORMATION CONTACT:

Peter Brierley,
Youth and Community Worker,
Christ Church,
576–580 Old Kent Road,
London,
SE15 1JF
Tel: 020 7732 5935
Email: hamiltonbrierley@hotmail.com

'It's really exciting to see these kids coming into a church building because that's where they want to be. This is a pretty needy area, but it's exciting to be a part of a church which is helping to meet the needs around us.'

SECTION 4:

Family

28. CARE – Pregnancy Crisis Centres

In 1985 the Pregnancy Crisis centre in Basingstoke opened, and two years later a second centre was launched in Southampton. Following this, other churches began to catch the vision and the number of centres began to grow. An umbrella organisation was set up to offer guidance and support, and in 1993 this became a department of CARE.

HOW IT WORKS

There are now more than 150 pregnancy crisis centres operating in the UK as part of the CARE Centres Network. CARE does not own any of the centres but serves each, offering support from planning to operation. The centres are united by their desire to express in a compassionate way God's heart concerning abortion, his care for all life however conceived, as well as his love and concern for the mother and father facing an unexpected pregnancy. A Christian Pregnancy Crisis Centre is a place where women can find people who care about them and their problems, offering a range of services that help them make the right decisions for them and their baby.

DEVELOPMENT

There is a universal need for the centres as they address universal concerns. CARE offers a comprehensive guide to setting up a centre and is looking for local churches to expand the reaches of its work.

THINGS TO CONSIDER

- Does your community already have a Christian Pregnancy Crisis Centre?
- Could you work in partnership with the CARE Centres

Network in offering this service in your area?

- Although setting up a centre would require lots of hard work, support is available from people who have considerable experience in this area. What's holding you back?

HOW TO GET FUNDING

As each centre is run separately, their funding comes from a variety of sources. The CARE Centres Network manual *Setting Up a Centre* contains details of how your centre might be funded.

FOR ADVICE AND MORE INFORMATION CONTACT:

Joanna Thompson,
CARE Centres Network,
1 Winton Square,
Basingstoke,
Hants,
RG21 8EN
Tel: 01256 477300
Fax: 01256 477301
Email: ccn@care.org.uk
Web: www.pregnancy.org.uk

'CARE Centres Network has a vision to provide accessible help to every person in the United Kingdom needing support in a crisis pregnancy or post-abortion situation through local centres and CARE CONFIDENTIAL, the national helpline.'

29. The Stopsley Project

A partnership between Stopsley Baptist Church and Spurgeon's Childcare, the Stopsley Project has been working in Luton for the last 15 years. The project aims to support families within the local community through a variety of initiatives. Focusing on family issues, principally parenting, the project seeks to enhance and enable stable family life.

HOW IT WORKS

The Stopsley Project offers a number of initiatives to help families. Parenting classes are offered both to parents of young children and those who have teenagers. These courses help parents to understand the importance of their role, as well as providing them with the resources and support to enjoy their task. In addition, several groups for parents with young children are run by the project. Two of these groups, Creative Capers and Mini Musicians, enable parents to interact with their children as they play and develop new skills through art, craft, music and communication.

DEVELOPMENT

The project is hoping to open a community café, around which other family-focused activities and support services will be provided, for example a lone parents group and IT activities.

THINGS TO CONSIDER

- What facilities are available for parents in your area?
- Could your church offer parenting courses? Remember that a wealth of course material is available from Parentalk and other sources.

- How might you integrate parents into existing schemes that your church runs for children?

HOW TO GET FUNDING

The parenting activities provided by the Stopsley Project are partly self-funded through nominal charges made for each participant. Health Action Zone, Luton, have provided a grant for three parenting courses to be run. The partnership between Stopsley Baptist Church and Spurgeon's Childcare facilitates the staffing and other running costs of the project.

FOR ADVICE AND MORE INFORMATION CONTACT:

The Stopsley Project,
Stopsley Baptist Church,
St Thomas' Road,
Luton,
Bedfordshire,
LU2 7XP
Tel: 01582 405293
Fax: 01582 418357
Email. office@stopsley.net
Web: www.stopsley.net

'Train your child in the way in which you know you should have gone yourself.' (Charles Spurgeon)

30. Avencare – Family Support Service

The Avencare project in Preston, Lancashire, provides social support to local people while at the same time building and developing a sense of community. Avencare was originally initiated in 1997 by Catholic Caring Services as part of their community development programme. The project is now jointly run by a local Roman Catholic church and an Anglican church.

HOW IT WORKS

Avencare's Family Support Service provides non-judgmental, confidential, free and friendly support to individuals and families in the Avenham area who, for whatever reason, have difficulty coping but do not fall into a category for which statutory help is available. The initiative helps a range of families and individuals, for example families of children at the local primary school who are not reaching their full educational potential as a result of difficulties at home, families who may need support to access information from other professional agencies, and parents with drug abuse problems. A family support worker is employed by Avencare to facilitate this work.

DEVELOPMENT

The Family Support Service plans to expand the support that it offers in order to reach more families in the area. Through developing existing relationships with statutory services it will be able to give more directed help to its clients.

THINGS TO CONSIDER

- Are families in your area falling through the gap of statutory care?
- What could your church do to meet their needs?
- What are the problems that people are facing, and how might you alleviate those problems?
- Could you commit to long-term relationships with struggling families or would it be better to provide short-term help?

HOW TO GET FUNDING

Avencare has applied to a range of funding sources to continue its work. These include: The Community Fund, The Home Office Family Support Grant, Local Community Chest, the Lancashire Children's Fund and a number of charitable trusts.

FOR ADVICE AND MORE INFORMATION CONTACT:

Joseph Cobb,
Avencare,
c/o The Foxton Centre,
Knowsley Street,
Preston,
Lancashire,
PR1 3SA
Tel: 01772 558404

'Avencare works closely with local organisations with an interest in its work, including faith groups and the wider community. It aims to contribute to the development and training of voluntary workers where possible.'

31. CARE – Remand Fostering

Inspired by a desire to see young offenders diverted from a lifetime in the criminal justice system, CARE instituted a system of remand fostering in 1998. The project places young offenders, who have been remanded to local authority accommodation, into the supportive environment of Christian families.

HOW IT WORKS

The remand fostering programme takes young people (aged 12–17) and aims to challenge them at every level – from thoughts, attitudes and values, to behaviour. The ultimate goal of the project is to rescue its charges from a life of crime and encourage positive development. This is achieved through both the support received in the foster home and a programme of daytime activities attended on a full-time basis, as well as breaking with established behaviour patterns and negative peer influences. There is a strong emphasis on equipping the young people for the future, supporting and enabling them to progress towards re-entering education or employment.

DEVELOPMENT

Initially the remand fostering project operated solely in Reading. However, plans to expand have been realised, with further schemes already operating in Birmingham and Basildon, Essex.

THINGS TO CONSIDER

- Are there families in your church who would be prepared to foster a difficult child – offering love, support and equality within the family?

- A project such as CARE's remand fostering requires a great knowledge of the local authority care structure. It might be too daunting to set up your own fostering programme, but could you work in partnership with an existing charity like CARE?

HOW TO GET FUNDING

The remand fostering programme is extremely expensive to run, costing £1,200 per young person per week. However, these costs are met entirely by the placing local authority, which also pays for clothing for the young people.

FOR ADVICE AND MORE INFORMATION CONTACT:

Tim Clewer,
P.O. Box 2169,
Reading,
Berkshire,
RG30 2FH
Tel: 0118 967 8440
Email: crf@care.org.uk
Web: www.remandfostering.org.uk

'Our aim is to provide young people with a stable environment that is designed to facilitate positive development.'

32. Romsey Mill – The Young Parent Project

The Young Parent Project at Romsey Mill began with a piece of research in the spring of 1997. From there it has grown and developed such that it now works with approximately 80 teenage mothers (as well as young women who were teenage parents) and is recognised as a lead provider for such support work across Cambridgeshire.

HOW IT WORKS

The Young Parent Project provides intensive support to teenage mothers as well as lone mothers who, having become parents in their teens, are now in their early twenties. Its purpose is to address the isolation, low self-esteem and low skill base of these young women. It sets out to do this by assisting them in developing the skills necessary to tackle the multiple disadvantages they face, in order to break the cycle of deprivation which so easily traps teenage parents. The project focuses on empowerment and helping its clients to look to the future. By providing individual, intensive support to encourage the development of confidence and life skills, it enables young mothers to re-enter education or the labour market.

DEVELOPMENT

Following the success of the Young Parent Project, there are plans to replicate the initiative in new locations elsewhere in the UK.

THINGS TO CONSIDER

- In what way could you help empower disadvantaged teenage mums in your community?

- How might you ensure that they did not feel judged or condemned by your church?
- What would your long-term goals be?

HOW TO GET FUNDING

Funding for the Young Parent Project has been secured for the next two years through grants from the European Social Fund, Comic Relief, Cambridgeshire Health Authority and Cambridge City Council.

FOR ADVICE AND MORE INFORMATION CONTACT:

Liz Diamond,
The Young Parent Project,
Romsey Mill Trust,
Hemingford Road,
Cambridge,
CB1 3BZ
Tel: 01223 566021
Fax: 01223 566092
Email: ypp@romseymill.org.uk
Web: www.romseymill.org.uk

'Romsey Mill Youth and Community Centre was set up in 1980 by local churches to meet the needs of the local community and in particular those of families and young people. We recognise that these needs are physical, social, emotional and spiritual.'

33. Cornerstone – Forever Fostering

Cornerstone is the fostering project of CARE – a national Christian charity. Based in the North East of England, the project was initiated in 1999 by a Christian couple on Teesside in order to recruit Christian foster carers who could provide loving and stable homes to sibling groups. CARE took over management of the project in 2002.

HOW IT WORKS

Cornerstone's aim is to improve the outcomes for children and young people in public care through the provision of a quality fostering service, while at the same time keeping siblings together. The children involved have all suffered emotionally, physically and psychologically and therefore can display very challenging behaviour. However, this does not deter Cornerstone from its objective of developing an expertise in providing and supporting the placement of sibling groups into what they call 'forever families' which refers to the concept of keeping brothers and sisters together beyond their time in the care of a local authority.

DEVELOPMENT

CARE is planning to replicate the Teesside model in other parts of the country. The vision for the future on Teesside includes the further recruitment of both long-term and respite foster families, as well as additional development of their Children's Counselling and Play Therapy Service.

THINGS TO CONSIDER

- Could your church work in partnership with CARE in its replication of Cornerstone across the country?

- Does your church have families who could take on two or more long-term foster children?

HOW TO GET FUNDING

The provision of foster care is very expensive. However, the local authorities have an obligation to house the children in their care and consequently offer comprehensive funding for children placed with families.

FOR ADVICE AND MORE INFORMATION CONTACT:

Cornerstone,
Annie House,
Master Road,
Thornaby,
Stockton-on-Tees,
TS17 0BE

Tel: 01642 751144
Fax: 01642 751133
Email: cornerstone@care.org.uk
Web: www.care.org.uk

'Perhaps the greatest social service that can be rendered by anybody to this country and to mankind is to bring up a family.'
(George Bernard Shaw)

34. Maybridge – Take a Break

Take a Break is a parent and toddler group that provides a regular, safe and welcoming environment for parents to find support and integration while their toddlers enjoy the stimulation of playing with other children. It also offers regular health promotion through visits from local health professionals.

HOW IT WORKS

Take a Break aims to provide a safe environment in which children can play while facilitating support networks for their parents. It looks to offer a well-rounded service, encouraging good parenting skills and running parenting courses to share problems and solutions. The children enjoy art, craft, song and dance, while healthcare is provided by health visitors and oral health workers. The MILE Project which runs Take a Break has found it to be central to their community work, acting as a hub from which other activities develop.

DEVELOPMENT

It is planned that Take a Break will grow through replication in other neighbourhoods within the local area. The project will also develop the training element of its work, offering comprehensive parenting skills classes and courses in first aid, quitting smoking, and drug awareness. These programmes will allow Take a Break to develop deeper relationships and afford greater opportunities to offer one-to-one advice. A family support worker may be appointed if need demands.

THINGS TO CONSIDER

- Could your church launch a similar scheme to Take a Break?

- What professional workers could you approach to run groups or information sessions within your existing mothers and toddlers club?
- Do you have larger schemes in your area that work with parents which you could link into?

HOW TO GET FUNDING

Take a Break is largely self-funded through small weekly subscriptions per family. However, the Primary Care Trust Health Promotion department provides a small grant as the group is promoting good health habits.

FOR ADVICE AND MORE INFORMATION CONTACT:

The MILE Project,
c/o Maybridge Community Church,
The Strand,
Maybridge,
Worthing,
West Sussex,
BN12 6DL
Tel: 01903 603337
Email: info@mile-project.org.uk
Web: www.mile-project.org.uk

'We feel so welcome, there are no cliques and everyone's really friendly.'

35. Care for the Family – Single Parent Network

Single Parents often express their desire to meet with other people in similar circumstances for support and social contact. As part of the wider support that Care for the Family offers lone parents, they have published a book, *Single Parents in Focus*, to provide local churches with insights and practical suggestions for supporting parents in this position.

HOW IT WORKS

Each local project that is part of the Single Parent Network develops as those involved feel is appropriate. In Crewe, for example, Christian single parents from various churches met together for some time. They developed a vision to reach other parents in similar situations. A drop-in centre was started one day a week, run by single parents for single parents. The centre provides a number of facilities, including an opportunity to meet with others, a counsellor, a thrift shop, a crèche with qualified staff, and information. Parenting, assertiveness and computer courses are also offered.

DEVELOPMENT

The Single Parent Network is soon to publish a Directory of Christian agencies, groups and individuals who offer a broad spectrum of support for single parents. It will also include other relevant sources of help and information. Plans are also being made to offer further training for the leaders of support groups.

THINGS TO CONSIDER

- What are the needs of single parents in your community?
- Could your church offer child care during the day to enable single parents to work and avoid the huge costs of existing child care structures?
- What other practical help and support could your church offer?
- Could your church work alongside Care for the Family and the Single Parents Network?

HOW TO GET FUNDING

Each project within the Single Parents Network is largely self-funded through donations, church support, grant-making trusts and other funding sources – Care for the Family underwrites the cost and makes up the balance of member groups.

FOR ADVICE AND MORE INFORMATION CONTACT:

Care for the Family,
Garth House,
Leon Avenue,
CARDIFF,
CF15 7RG
Tel: 029 2081 0800
Fax: 029 2081 4089
Email: mail@cff.org.uk
Web: www.care-for-the-family.org.uk

'Parenting alone is one of the hardest tasks in the world and our aim in the Single Parent team is to bring encouragement and support.'

36. Maybridge – Well Baby Clinic

The health visitors at the local GP surgery in Maybridge were approached by the MILE Project regarding the setting up of a partnership to run a Well Baby Clinic as a health promotion outreach service. The resulting project has been running successfully since June 2001.

HOW IT WORKS

The Well Baby Clinic aims to provide an environment that will foster the building of friendships between local parents, while at the same time offering a necessary medical service. It provides a child-friendly environment which also supports parents with information, advice and relevant resources. The location of the clinic makes it easily accessible, providing a central meeting point for parents and health professionals. This interaction has dual benefit as it also affords the medical staff with a deeper understanding of the local community and its needs.

DEVELOPMENT

Though there are currently no firm plans to further develop this project, the staff are constantly looking for ways of improving and extending the service they provide.

THINGS TO CONSIDER

- Are your premises child-friendly?
- Is the venue suitable for confidential sessions?
- Are your local GPs interested in working in partnership with you?

HOW TO GET FUNDING

Maybridge Community Church currently subsidises the cost of using the hall. The Strand Surgery provides health visitors and their equipment for professional advice. West Sussex Health Authority provides small grants for resources such as health screens and baby mats.

FOR ADVICE AND MORE INFORMATION CONTACT:

The MILE Project
c/o Maybridge Community Church,
The Strand,
Maybridge,
Worthing,
West Sussex,
BN12 6DL
Tel: 01903 603337
Email: info@mile-project.org.uk
Web: www.mile-project.org.uk

'It's a great place to come. They really help you out and take so much stress out of being a mum . . . I don't know what I would do without them.'

37. Care for the Family – Real Life Training

Real Life Training is designed to equip individuals to set up and run small group courses on marriage and parenting in the local community and has been developed in response to requests from people who want to use Care for the Family resources more effectively. In essence the courses are helping people to help others.

HOW IT WORKS

The project offers training in small-group facilitation skills, and provides two specially written five-session courses that have been developed around the *Sixty Minute Marriage* video and the *Parentalk Parenting Principles* video course. Both these courses are particularly suitable for use in the wider community as well as in the church. The programme is for anyone with a strong desire to strengthen and support families in their area. Real Life Training is not about becoming a parenting or marriage 'expert', as all the teaching is contained on video, but it is about becoming skilled as the person who can 'make it happen'. Real Life Training features an initial two-day residential training course, Bringing Life to Small Groups, where participants will learn and practise effective facilitation skills. Ongoing support and other benefits are also offered.

DEVELOPMENT

Real Life Training will be running regular Bringing Life to Small Groups courses throughout 2003 and beyond.

THINGS TO CONSIDER

- Could your church consider running parenting and/or marriage courses?

- Who in your church would run the courses?
- Would it be helpful to have course-specific training for those people?
- How might a project like this benefit your local community?

HOW TO GET FUNDING

The Real Life Training programme is largely self-funded. However, any shortfall is made up by Care for the Family.

FOR ADVICE AND MORE INFORMATION CONTACT:

Care for the Family,
Garth House,
Leon Avenue,
CARDIFF,
CF15 7RG
Tel: 029 2081 0800
Fax: 029 2081 4089
Email: mail@cff.org.uk
Web: www.care-for-the-family.org.uk

'Our task is to get alongside people in the good times and also in the tough times – bringing hope, compassion and some practical, down-to-earth encouragement.'

38. Dearne Valley Dads

DVD is a project for young fathers or father figures (aged 16–25 years) and their children across the South Yorkshire Coalfields area. The project essentially seeks to improve the mental, physical and emotional well-being of young fathers and their children, by promoting and encouraging the father's involvement with his child.

HOW IT WORKS

The Dearne Valley Dads project aims to support, educate and advise young fathers, assisting them to play a more active role in the parenting of their children. Outreach workers highlight the importance of the role of the father in the parenting of the child and the benefits of his involvement, as well as educating young men by raising the awareness of the issues of fatherhood. Young fathers are encouraged to develop a self-supporting peer group in order to lessen their feelings of isolation, share their experiences, be heard and listened to, learn new skills, build confidence and learn how to spend quality time with their children.

DEVELOPMENT

DVD is developing learning resources about 'fatherhood and the roles of the father' for young people and youth workers.

THINGS TO CONSIDER

- How might you help young men consider the role of fatherhood?
- How might your church positively model fatherhood?
- What support could your church offer to young fathers?
- What activities or events could you set up to enable or encourage fathers to spend more time with their children?

HOW TO GET FUNDING

DVD is funded through a Department of Health grant which was awarded to research and meet young fathers' need for support.

FOR ADVICE AND MORE INFORMATION CONTACT:

Nigel Rose,
YMCA,
Room 65, TTC Block,
Dearne Valley College,
Manvers Park,
Wath-upon-Dearne,
Rotherham,
S63 7EW
Tel: 01709 513350
Fax: 01709 838666
Email: young.dads@rotherham.ymca.org.uk

'It's hard when you have a kid and you're just a kid yourself . . . it's a big responsibility, but I'm taking this more seriously than I've ever taken anything – I'm going to be a good dad.'

39. Banbury Homes – Rachel House

Teenage pregnancy is a perennial problem which can only be eradicated through education. However, the standard arguments for the alleviation of the problem do little to help its victims. Rachel House, a Banbury Homes project, offers full-time practical help and housing to teenage girls who are pregnant or who have already become mothers.

HOW IT WORKS

Rachel House aims to provide accommodation for eleven mothers and babies who are in housing need. But more than that, the residents benefit from a high level of support which is provided 24/7 by a team of skilled and experienced staff. Rachel House is the only project of its kind in the area and draws its residents from across the county and sometimes further afield. Pregnant girls and young mothers (aged 16–25) are usually referred to the project by their local statutory services. Once resident they are offered advice and education in matters concerning pregnancy, birth and child care. They are also given education and training, through which they gain the confidence to live independently.

DEVELOPMENT

Rachel House aims to establish a benchmark standard for the whole country. Through its high level of standard practice it hopes to lead the way for others to follow, achieving excellence in the care of young mothers.

THINGS TO CONSIDER

- What could your church do to support young mothers?
- How might you combat the perception that the church is a

place of judgement rather than love?

- Could your church operate a project like Rachel House? Perhaps you could house teenage mothers with families within your church.

HOW TO GET FUNDING

Rachel House is funded both by rent from its residents and a grant from Supporting People. As with all of Banbury Homes' projects, the local church has been a considerable source of support, not least financially.

FOR ADVICE AND MORE INFORMATION CONTACT:

Rachel House,
Banbury Homes,
58 George Street,
Banbury,
OX16 5BH
Tel: 01295 265439
Email: DRG@banburyhomes.org.uk

'Rachel House is a pioneering new scheme to give young mothers the support and skills they need to take control of their lives and to care for their babies.'

40. Parentalk Events and Courses

Parenting can be a daunting experience. At no other point in our lives do we shoulder so much responsibility with so little training. Parentalk exists to inspire and equip parents at every stage of parenthood and has developed a range of resources designed to help ordinary mums and dads with the everyday joys and challenges that parenting brings.

HOW IT WORKS

The Parentalk Course is a video-based course for small groups, designed to bring mums and dads together to talk about common parenting issues and learn from one another. Laughter and the swapping of stories and experiences play a key part in each of the sessions as parents realise that they are not on their own and that they're not the only ones who struggle. The course addresses the problems and concerns of parents – empowering and enabling them to be better parents. There are currently some 3,000 Parentalk groups in operation around the UK.

DEVELOPMENT

Parentalk continues to launch new resources and services for parents and those who wish to impact families in their community. Its website (www.parentalk.co.uk) and the extensive range of Parentalk books act as useful and accessible follow-up tools. Additionally the organisation is working hard to formalise links with local communities as part of its regional strategy (information available directly from Parentalk).

THINGS TO CONSIDER

- What facilities are available for parents in your area?
- Could your church offer Parentalk courses to your community?

- Could your church host a Parentalk evening event to kick-start the initiative and attract new families?
- How could you expand this service beyond your church to the community?

HOW TO GET FUNDING

Each Parentalk pack, containing everything you need to run a course for up to ten people, costs £49.95 (plus P&P). Parentalk events vary in price, depending on your requirements. Funding is available from a range of sources, including statutory bodies and grant-making trusts.

FOR ADVICE AND MORE INFORMATION CONTACT:

Parentalk,
P.O. Box 23142,
London,
SE1 0ZT
Tel: 020 7450 9073
Email: info@parentalk.co.uk
Web: www.parentalk.co.uk

'Parentalk has helped my community to be empowered and supported in parenting. It has helped them to be equipped to love their children more. It has been a great resource for the church in building bridges into the community.'

SECTION 5:

Counselling, Mentoring

41. Community Chaplaincy

Community Chaplaincy projects, promoted and developed by the Churches Criminal Justice Forum, offer help to those leaving prison who do not have the benefit of supportive family ties. Their goal is the successful reintegration of ex-offenders back into the community.

HOW IT WORKS

The aim of Community Chaplaincy is to reduce re-offending as well as to assist ex-offenders in leading more settled and fulfilled lives. Volunteers who are recruited from local churches receive training and supervision. Contact usually begins when the prisoner is approaching his or her release date, and may continue once or twice a week for some months after it has taken place. The projects (which are running around the UK) have met with considerable success: for instance, in its first eleven months the Swansea team supported 91 prisoners. Only nine re-offended and were returned to the prison during this time – far below the national average.

DEVELOPMENT

So far local schemes are operating in Swansea, Gloucester, Preston and Nottingham; others are being developed in Bristol, North Staffordshire, Cardiff and Birmingham. The hope is that all local prisons will eventually benefit from a scheme in their area.

THINGS TO CONSIDER

- Would your church be able to work in partnership with the Churches Criminal Justice Forum to set up a project like this in your area?

HOW TO GET FUNDING

Funding and other resources have been obtained from a variety of sources, including local authorities, the police, the prison service, churches and charitable trusts.

FOR ADVICE AND MORE INFORMATION CONTACT:

Majors Lawrie and Angie Brown,
Community Chaplaincy Office,
The Salvation Army,
Birmingham Citadel Corps,
St Chads,
Queensway,
Birmingham,
B4 6HH
Tel: 0121 212 2825
Email: lawrie.brown@salvationarmy.org.uk

'[The Salvation Army's] mission is to proclaim his gospel, to persuade people of all ages to become his disciples and to engage in a programme of practical concern for the needs of humanity.'

42. Open Door, High Wycombe

Open Door is in essence a professional counselling facility, offering support, guidance and genuine solutions to the problems of its clients. Although it originally provided its service for a single session each week, rising numbers demanded a second weekly session. The centre now operates for five hours a week, during which time it serves on average 30 people.

HOW IT WORKS

Meeting people with such needs as loneliness, social isolation, addiction, homelessness and mental health issues, Open Door's voluntary staff (including professionals such as GPs and social workers from local churches) aim to support people as they re-establish themselves in the community. In many cases continued contact is maintained as clients return to work. Though not an explicit objective of the programme, some of those helped by the centre choose to join an Alpha course and go on to find ongoing support within the church family.

DEVELOPMENT

The Open Door team have recently opened a Saturday café. Operating from church premises, the café offers sandwiches and speciality coffees at minimal cost. Also available are shower and laundry facilities and the chance for those in need to have a substantial meal.

THINGS TO CONSIDER

- Is a counselling service operated by another church in your area?
- Do you have trained counsellors in your church? If not, are there people who are keen to receive training?

HOW TO GET FUNDING

Open Door has been largely self-funded, although it received a £500 grant from a local Primary Care group to assist with set-up costs. Links with Bucks Mental Health Trust have led to their support of the project and payment for one of the two weekly sessions.

FOR ADVICE AND MORE INFORMATION CONTACT:

Open Door,
The Hub, Union Baptist Church,
Easton Street,
High Wycombe,
Bucks,
HP11 1NJ

Tel/Fax: 01494 473889
Email: thehub@unionbaptist.org
Web: www.unionbaptist.org

'God has really blessed us and our work but continually challenges us about integration with the church . . . we hope to show that Christianity is more than a set of imposed structures.'

43. Crossroads Christian Counselling Service

CCCS is a professional counselling service providing help and support for residents of Tower Hamlets who are facing difficulties and need to talk. The service is aimed at those on low incomes who would be unable to afford or travel to alternative services. CCCS is a member of the British Association for Counselling and Psychotherapy.

HOW IT WORKS

The aim of counselling is to provide an opportunity for the client to work towards living in a more satisfying and resourceful way. CCCS is described as a Christian service because it is managed by local churches and staffed by Christians. It is distinctive because it offers whole person health care, giving an opportunity for people to explore emotional and spiritual issues. However, it makes no attempt to convert its clients, giving them full ownership of what is discussed in sessions.

DEVELOPMENT

CCCS has been offering a service for eight years. It relocated 18 months ago from a church building basement to a high street shop. This has increased accessibility and the public profile, as well as giving space for future expansion. A new child therapy service for 3–11-year-olds has been started in a local primary school.

THINGS TO CONSIDER

- What services are available to people struggling with mental health issues in your area?
- Given that statutory provision of ongoing mental health care

is limited and often targeted at those with serious psychiatric illness, is there a need for a counselling service in your area?

- What kind of service could you offer (counselling, prayer, friendship?) and to whom? (Those with an openness to the Christian faith, or anyone needing help?)

HOW TO GET FUNDING

CCCS receives over 50 per cent of its funding from regular giving by supporters and one-off gifts; 9 per cent is generated by client fees, which operate on a sliding scale linked to earnings. The balance is made up by fundraising events and grants.

FOR ADVICE AND MORE INFORMATION CONTACT:

Kim Gooding,
CCCS Office,
144 Roman Road,
Bethnal Green,
London,
E2 0RY
Tel: 020 8981 8388

'I find volunteering so valuable. It is a way for me to actively support the excellent service of CCCS and I can see the tangible results of the work I do, whether answering the telephone, working on a database or making a cup of tea.'

44. The Stopsley Project

The Stopsley Project has been working in Luton for the last 15 years as a partnership between Stopsley Baptist Church and Spurgeon's Childcare. The project aims to support families within the local community through a variety of initiatives. Focusing on family issues, principally parenting, the project seeks to enhance and enable stable family life.

HOW IT WORKS

Working solely with families with children, counselling constitutes a major part of the work of the Stopsley Project. The service deals with the feelings of loss generated by a variety of situations. Bereavement, unemployment (e.g. loss of status, income and self-esteem), marriage breakdown and divorce, and behavioural problems in children (which constitute a loss of control) are regular subjects raised by families in counselling sessions. The Stopsley Project aims to offer 'appropriate intervention' and consequently counsels both parents and children. Often counselling sessions with children focus on relieving the burden of guilt felt for things which are not their fault, especially in the case of the breakdown of marriage, and helping them to accept and negotiate the need for boundaries.

DEVELOPMENT

The Stopsley Project is hoping to develop a team of counsellors to enhance its service to families. The counselling service will continue to meet with families who are struggling with issues surrounding loss.

THINGS TO CONSIDER

- What counselling facilities are available in your area?
- Could your church be involved in counselling families struggling with loss?
- What training and skills would your counsellors need?
- Could you work in partnership with other groups/churches to work in this area?

HOW TO GET FUNDING

The Stopsley Project is a partnership between Stopsley Baptist Church and Spurgeon's Childcare. The partnership facilitates the staffing and running cost of the project. In the future the project may look to gain funding from other sources to further develop its service to families.

FOR ADVICE AND MORE INFORMATION CONTACT:

The Stopsley Project,
Stopsley Baptist Church,
St Thomas' Road,
Luton,
Bedfordshire,
LU2 7XP
Tel: 01582 405293
Fax: 01582 418357
Email: office@stopsley.net
Web: www.stopsley.net

'Do not measure your loss by itself; if you do, it will seem intolerable; but if you will take all human affairs into account you will find that some comfort is to be derived from them.'
(Saint Basil)

45. Family Matters, Luton

Family Matters was established in 1995 as an innovative response to issues of domestic violence in the local area. The project, working with local health practitioners, counsels both the victims and perpetrators of domestic violence. Family Matters is working to address an issue that affects many people, dealing with anger, stress and lack of self-confidence.

HOW IT WORKS

The ultimate goal of Family Matters is to end the pattern of abuse in the home. This can be achieved by working with either the victim (re-establishing self-worth and offering practical steps towards defusing a situation of violence) or the aggressor (dealing with the root causes of anger and offering alternatives to violence – even if this is simply walking it off!). Through the process of empowering the victim and re-educating the aggressor, Family Matters has seen relationships transformed. The project draws on a mixture of pastoral approaches and clinical insights, though at its heart its work follows biblical models of Christian counselling.

DEVELOPMENT

Family Matters is expanding its range of services to offer more holistic help to the whole family unit. The project now offers parenting courses, a parents' forum, a mental health initiative and an achievement project called 'Black Boys Can'.

THINGS TO CONSIDER

- Is there an unmet need relating to domestic violence counselling in your area?
- Does your church have trained counsellors?

- What facilities would you need to set up an effective service?

HOW TO GET FUNDING

Family Matters receives some revenue from the charges it makes for each counselling session – however, these nominal fees do not cover its costs. Further funding has been received from local churches as well as Christian charities. Some funding has also come from the local council and the Single Regeneration Budget.

FOR ADVICE AND MORE INFORMATION CONTACT:

Pastor Trevor Adams,
Family Matters,
27 Axe Close,
Luton,
Bedfordshire,
LU3 3LT
Tel: 01582 651011
Fax: 01582 598148

To read more about Family Matters see *Faithworks: Stories of Hope.*

'One client went home and said to her partner, "If you ever touch me again, you will never see me or the kids a0gain." The simple shock of her standing up for the first time initiated a complete change in that relationship.'

46. Oasis Youth Inclusion Schools Mentoring – Primary Transition

The transition from primary to secondary school can be one of the most stressful and unsettling times in a young person's life. Oasis Youth Inclusion's primary transitional work aims to prepare and support pupils who might struggle at this time and who might later face exclusion.

HOW IT WORKS

The Youth Inclusion team starts working with the children in the spring term of their final year at primary school. Working in groups, such issues as behaviour management, self-esteem and self-control are addressed. In the summer term the group work focuses upon the practical aspects of the move to secondary school. Regular one-to-one meetings between the pupils and the group worker allow the children to discuss issues that they would not want to raise in the group setting. During the summer break, students who still seem likely to have problems making the transition are offered ongoing mentoring in their homes. From this the mentors can build a rapport with the whole family unit. The final phase of the programme aims to provide one-to-one support for the pupils during their first term at secondary school.

DEVELOPMENT

It is hoped that in the future the programme will go into an increasing number of schools.

THINGS TO CONSIDER

- Does anyone else offer a mentoring programme to schools in your area?

- What other projects does your church run? How might a youth inclusion project interrelate with these?
- Do you have existing staff who are skilled or experienced in youth inclusion work, or will others need to be recruited or trained?
- Could you work with Oasis Youth Inclusion to set up a programme in your community?

HOW TO GET FUNDING

Oasis Youth Inclusion receives funding from a range of sources. These include DfES and Connexions, Children in Need, the Neighbourhood Renewal Fund and the Children's Fund. Statutory funding from 'On Track' also supports the work carried out in primary schools.

FOR ADVICE AND MORE INFORMATION CONTACT:

Pietro Battista,
Oasis Youth Inclusion,
The Oasis Centre,
115 Southwark Bridge Road,
London,
SE1 0AX
Tel: 020 7450 9000
Email: Pietro.battista@oasistrust.org
Web: www.oasistrust.org

'I have enjoyed the group a lot. It was excellent, brilliant, fantastic . . . I have learned to control my temper. I have also enjoyed speaking to the course leaders . . . the course has made me more confident and positive in whatever I do.'

47. Oasis Youth Inclusion Schools Mentoring – Secondary Support

The exclusion of young people from school is a growing problem which manifests itself in two ways. Excluded children are either forced out of full-time education because of their behaviour (fighting, etc.) or they withdraw from school of their own volition (truanting). The Youth Inclusion team at Oasis is working to reverse these trends.

HOW IT WORKS

Oasis Youth Inclusion offers support to secondary school pupils in two ways: group work and one-to-one mentoring. Group work is offered to small groups of young people (typically 6–8) or occasionally to whole classes. These groups provide an opportunity to discuss social, emotional, relational, behavioural and family issues. They tend to meet for a whole academic year, allowing the participants to bond together. The one-to-one mentoring provides support for those who might not be suited to group work or who require additional support. The one-to-one nature of the sessions enables the mentoring relationship to be targeted to specific needs. Oasis Youth Inclusion provides mentors who work alongside individuals who are highlighted by the school as being at risk of exclusion.

DEVELOPMENT

Oasis Youth Inclusion currently works with around 30 secondary schools. It aims to further its work by moving into more schools and working with more young people.

THINGS TO CONSIDER

- What support is currently given to those at risk of exclusion in your area?
- Do you have existing staff who are skilled or experienced in youth inclusion work, or will others need to be recruited or trained?
- Could you work in partnership with Oasis Youth Inclusion to set up a programme in your community?

HOW TO GET FUNDING

Oasis Youth Inclusion receives funding from a range of sources. These include DfES and Connexions, Children in Need, the Neighbourhood Renewal Fund and the Children's Fund.

FOR ADVICE AND MORE INFORMATION CONTACT:

Pietro Battista,
Oasis Youth Inclusion,
The Oasis Centre,
115 Southwark Bridge Road,
London,
SE1 0AX
Tel: 020 7450 9000
Email: Pietro.battista@oasistrust.org
Web: www.oasistrust.org

'I enjoyed every part of the group because it has been easier to talk and get to know each other better . . . my temper has calmed down a lot and I have hardly been in trouble since the group.'

48. The Bereaved Parents Network

The Bereaved Parents Network (BPN) was launched by Care for the Family in autumn 1999, in response to the needs of parents who have suffered the loss of a son or daughter. The main area of help BPN offers is a telephone befriending service. New clients are put in touch with an existing member of the network who is a committed Christian and a bereaved parent themselves.

HOW IT WORKS

Barbie Reynolds (one of the founders of the project) says of the telephone befrienders: 'If you have been through that pain and desolation of loss, you can identify with others who are going through the same experience. You have to work through your own pain to then be able to help others.' Alongside telephone befriending, the network holds a series of day events just for bereaved parents – a chance to be with others in similar circumstances, learning about handling loss and grief and how to make a way forward.

DEVELOPMENT

In 2002 the first weekend for bereaved siblings (aged 16–25) was held. For many of these young adults it was the first time they had been able to talk freely about their grief and be with others who could identify with them.

THINGS TO CONSIDER

- What services for the bereaved are already available in your area?
- In what way could your church offer help to those who are coping with bereavement?

- Could your church work in partnership with Care for the Family in its work with bereaved parents?
- What facilities would you need to set up a project such as the Bereaved Parents Network?

HOW TO GET FUNDING

The Bereaved Parents Network is supported by funding from the Family Policy Unit of the Home Office.

FOR ADVICE AND MORE INFORMATION CONTACT:

Care for the Family,
Garth House,
Leon Avenue,
CARDIFF,
CF15 7RG
Tel: 029 2081 0800
Fax: 029 2081 4089
Email: mail@cff.org.uk
Web: www.care-for-the-family.org.uk

'For the first time we felt like someone really, really understood.'

49. African-Caribbean Achievement Project

ACAP is a mentoring project set up in response to the concerns of African-Caribbean parents in the City of Bradford. A disturbing trend of underachievement among black boys had been observed – although they did well at primary school, this tailed off dramatically in secondary education. ACAP provides positive black role models to children of all ages.

HOW IT WORKS

The aim of ACAP is simply to help those children it mentors achieve their potential within the education system. The students are introduced to a black person who is an achiever in industry, commerce, the arts or sport. In primary schools this mentor works with a whole class; with older children, however, one-to-one relationships are fostered. The mentoring programme operates alongside supplementary schooling on Saturdays. The overall focus of ACAP is to promote education as a fun and rewarding pursuit. Through positive role models and innovative learning programmes, previously disruptive students are more motivated and consequently more likely to do well at school.

DEVELOPMENT

The future aim of ACAP is that the service it provides should no longer be necessary – that ACAP's good practice should become standard practice in all schools.

THINGS TO CONSIDER

- What provision is made for those underachieving in schools in your area?
- How might your church be involved in breaking the cycle of underachievement?

- How might you provide positive role models?

HOW TO GET FUNDING

ACAP is currently funded by the Children's Fund, with help from Education Bradford. However, in the future the project will be funded by Education Bradford as part of their Education Development Plan.

FOR ADVICE AND MORE INFORMATION CONTACT:

Tony Parry,
CANA Project Leader,
31 Moor Road,
Headingley,
Leeds,
LS6 4BG
Tel: 0113 274 4940
Fax: 0113 274 4942
Email: Tony.parry@barnardos.org.uk

'What we're doing should already be standard practice in schools . . . you can break the cycle of underachievement and we just want to get that message across.'

50. GreenHouse Mentoring, Luton

Stopsley Baptist Church has developed a programme of mentoring young people within the schools of Luton. The children to be mentored are identified by local schools. For instance they might exhibit anger problems, be a victim of bullying, lack self-confidence – or any other issue that hinders their progress and enjoyment of school. Mentors act as a friend, listening ear and positive role model.

HOW IT WORKS

Although we delight in telling the young that school days are the best of their lives, for many this could not be further from the truth. The mentoring project aims to offer support to children for whom school is a difficult environment. Through regular meetings with a mentor, behavioural issues are addressed and social skills are developed; the children are encouraged to realise their potential and nourished in order to grow. The mentor and child meet weekly for around an hour over a period of 1–2 years. Over the course of these relationships radical transformations are often witnessed.

DEVELOPMENT

In the future the project aims to focus on the special needs of asylum seekers, increase the number of schools in which it works, and address the problem of transition from primary to secondary school.

THINGS TO CONSIDER

- What are the specific needs of the children in your area?
- How many mentors are potentially available to you?
- Are you willing to be involved long term?

- Is mentoring already operating in schools? What form does this take? Will your work help or hinder existing projects?
- What age group will you work with?

HOW TO GET FUNDING

The GreenHouse Mentoring Project is funded by the Children's Fund through a service agreement with the council. You might also consider approaching children's charities and grant-making trusts. Although a project like this need not be hugely demanding financially, its time demands are great.

FOR ADVICE AND MORE INFORMATION CONTACT:

Chloe Stirling-Smith,
GreenHouse Mentoring,
The GreenHouse,
16–22 St Thomas' Road,
Luton,
Beds,
LU2 7UY
Tel: 01582 898883
Email: chloe@stopsley.net

'Mentoring is a valuable opportunity to encourage young people to reach their potential. The relationships we have established are transforming lives – it is exciting to see the work develop.'

51. Maybridge – The Fuse

The Fuse is an after-school club running once a week between 2.45–4.15 p.m. specifically aimed at pupils identified as being 'at risk' of exclusion from school. The focus is on children undergoing the difficult transition between first and middle school. The ethos of the group is to encourage change through rewarding good behaviour with trips and outings away from Maybridge.

HOW IT WORKS

Simply stated, the aim of The Fuse is to reduce the number of children excluded from mainstream education, thus avoiding the cycle of problems associated with exclusion from school. Practically this is achieved by mentoring those pupils identified as being at risk of exclusion, fostering positive behaviour patterns in disruptive children. The Fuse takes a holistic approach to the problem of disruptive children, visiting the families in question to encourage an ongoing supportive environment, thus reducing the chances of exclusion later in school life.

DEVELOPMENT

The Fuse plans to expand its service with more groups running in its existing schools. A mediation service is in the pipeline, offering support for parents when dealing with the school or other statutory bodies concerning their child. A new after-school project will be established to support pupils after they have made the transition between schools. A new youth worker may be employed to fulfil these ambitions.

THINGS TO CONSIDER

- What links does your church have with local schools that might enable you to suggest a project like The Fuse?
- How might you monitor the success of the project, and how will you ascertain improvements in child behaviour?
- How would you approach parents to involve them in this process?

HOW TO GET FUNDING

Maybridge Community Church currently subsidises The Fuse Project Manager and provides the premises used. West Sussex Drugs Action Team Innovation Fund 2002/3 has provided a small grant for resources. Further funding has been received from West Sussex Social Services through their 'Pump Priming New Projects' grant.

FOR ADVICE AND MORE INFORMATION CONTACT:

The MILE Project,
c/o Maybridge Community Church,
The Strand,
Maybridge,
Worthing,
West Sussex,
BN12 6DL
Tel: 01903 603337
Email: info@mile-project.org.uk
Web: www.mile-project.org.uk

'In terms of these children's lives the relationship made with the adults at The Fuse must be seen as one huge positive factor. They will be the only positive relationships the children have with any form of formal organisation and this will support them through the transfer of schools.'

52. Oasis Youth Inclusion – Community Mentoring

Oasis Youth Inclusion's work in the community began in response to an identified need with young people at risk of social exclusion outside of the school environment. Within most communities there are disaffected young people who would benefit from mentoring, without which they may be drawn into a downward cycle of anti-social behaviour.

HOW IT WORKS

In every community which sees young people hanging around on street corners and getting into trouble with residents, businesses and the police, there is a need for mentoring – a need which can be met by the church. Most churches could run a community-based mentoring programme. Volunteers are recruited to act as mentors and, following training and the necessary police checks, are placed in a mentoring relationship with a young person. The mentor simply acts as a positive role model, friend and encourager – for many of the youngsters their mentor is the only Christian in their life. The relationship normally lasts for one year, with participants meeting once a fortnight, outside of school.

DEVELOPMENT

Oasis is keen to help more community mentoring projects develop. For more information on how your church might be involved, contact Oasis Youth Inclusion.

THINGS TO CONSIDER

- Is there a need for a community-based mentoring programme in your area?

- Do you have a pool of potential volunteers able and willing to be trained to work with young people?
- What specific aims and objectives do you wish to accomplish?

HOW TO GET FUNDING

Oasis Youth Inclusion receives funding from a range of sources. These include DfES and Connexions, Children in Need, the Neighbourhood Renewal Fund and the Children's Fund.

FOR ADVICE AND MORE INFORMATION CONTACT:

Pietro Battista,
Oasis Youth Inclusion,
The Oasis Centre,
115 Southwark Bridge Road,
London,
SE1 0AX
Tel: 020 7450 9000
Email: Pietro.battista@oasistrust.org
Web: www.oasistrust.org

'I went into the mentoring relationship looking to help my mentee. But I have been amazed at how inspired and challenged I have been personally at seeing one person grow and be impacted so much, simply by being in a relationship.'

SECTION 6:

Employment

53. City Gateway

London's Brick Lane forms a boundary between the city's rich and poor – to the west there is great prosperity, to the east some of the greatest poverty. To the largely Bengali population of Spitalfields, the city of London with its countless job opportunities is a closed world. City Gateway is helping the poor find work in the city.

HOW IT WORKS

The City Gateway process begins with training – each of the long-term unemployed students is taught computer skills. The twelve-week long courses – the European Computer Driving Licence and Certified Internet Webmaster – run alongside an employment preparation course presented in partnership with city firms and boast an 80 per cent pass rate. Following this training, each student is given a four-week placement with a company in the city. The placements are very important in developing practical experience in the workplace, as the students are often from families which have survived solely on benefits, and to whom a nine-to-five job is an alien concept.

DEVELOPMENT

The project has constantly developed since it started in 1999, now offering courses in Web Design and Maintenance, and in 2003 the launch of a flexible development training course which incorporates outdoor pursuits with IT training.

THINGS TO CONSIDER

- Is there a large gap between the rich and poor in your area?
- What needs to be done to narrow that gap?
- Is a project like City Gateway appropriate for your area?

HOW TO GET FUNDING

Tearfund and the Mercers Company initially funded City Gateway. However, as it has grown it has received funding from the European Social Fund and the Single Regeneration Budget. Deutsche Bank also contributes, providing the salary of one member of staff.

FOR ADVICE AND MORE INFORMATION CONTACT:

City Gateway,
Bethnal Green Training Centre,
Hanbury Street,
London,
E1 5HZ
Tel: 020 7247 2202
Fax: 020 7247 2204
Email: info@citygateway.org.uk
Web: www.citygateway.org.uk

To read more about the City Gateway story see *Faithworks: Stories of Hope.*

'The barriers to professional employment are huge. Entering a nine-to-five working culture is a massive cultural leap for someone from three generations of unemployment, who is used to living off the dole and various other benefits.'

54. The Gate Arts Centre

The Gate is a centre for expression and training in the arts which allows people to explore their innate, God-given creativity. Although The Gate has a clear Christian basis, it is committed to being inclusive and has no sectarian bias or proselytising agenda.

HOW IT WORKS

The Gate not only runs an art centre which is open to anyone in the community who would like to develop their artistic gifts, but has also launched a personal development project. Working in two local schools and a prison, the project runs courses for those who are at risk of long-term unemployment and social disaffection. These courses aim to help young people and adults develop their natural skills, enabling them to make the most of their opportunities and informed choices about their future. Students are encouraged to develop skills that can easily be transferred into the workplace making them more attractive to potential employers.

DEVELOPMENT

The Gate is keen to reach as wide an audience as possible and is constantly looking for innovative ways to use the arts, educate people and help them reach their full potential.

THINGS TO CONSIDER

- How could your church use the arts to help people realise their potential?
- What specialist skill and facilities might you need in order to start a project like The Gate?

- Does your church have people who could help others to develop their artistic gifts?

HOW TO GET FUNDING

The Gate Arts Centre has received funding from a variety of sources both from the private and public sector, including the European Social Fund and Heritage Lottery Foundation. Gifts of services and money from individuals and companies have also been a considerable source of support.

FOR ADVICE AND MORE INFORMATION CONTACT:

The Gate Trust,
136 Newport Road,
Cardiff,
CF24 1DJ
Tel: 029 2045 1000
Fax: 029 2045 9900
Email: info@gateartscentre.co.uk
Web: www.gateartscentre.co.uk

'Our aim is to change attitudes towards education, the arts and faith, and to show positive examples of Christians serving the community.'

55. Holme Christian Care Centre

Originally operating as a project for the unemployed, giving access to job vacancies, the Holme Christian Care Centre has grown beyond all measure. It was soon realised that unemployed people needed more than information about available jobs; they needed education to enable them to secure and retain work. The centre now offers comprehensive care.

HOW IT WORKS

Operating from 9.00 a.m. to 5.30 p.m. every Monday to Thursday, the education and training department of the Holme Christian Care Centre runs 50 courses a week in the centre's fully equipped IT suites. These courses lead to formal qualifications in a range of subjects: everything from typing to child care. Many people have found employment as a result of the time invested in them by Holme. Further to education though, the centre offers child care for 150 children a week, support for the elderly and disabled adults with a range of activities, an advice service, as well as a youth project which works through a drop-in centre, in local schools and on the streets.

DEVELOPMENT

A project like Holme Christian Care Centre, which began as a small local church initiative but has grown into a significant community facility, is a clear example of how a small idea can develop.

THINGS TO CONSIDER

- If you could address one need in your community, what would it be?

- How might you expand on that idea to reach more people and meet more needs?
- What would you imagine your project looking like in ten years' time?
- How can you go about making that vision happen?

HOW TO GET FUNDING

The Holme Christian Care Centre receives funding from a range of sources including the European Regional Development Fund, Church Urban Fund, BBC Children in Need, and Tearfund, among many other strategic partnerships.

FOR ADVICE AND MORE INFORMATION CONTACT:

Revd Alan Evans,
Holme Christian Care Centre,
Madison Avenue,
Holmewood,
Bradford,
BD4 9RY
Tel: 01274 689306
Fax: 01274 653332
Email: holme.christian_carecentre@virgin.net

'Our desire is to show the love of Jesus in practical, caring ways, and through our endeavours enable and encourage people to grow in confidence.'

SECTION 7:

Debt, Economic Hardship

56. Unafund

Unafund is a charity which grants interest-free loans to people who are threatened with losing their home. Understanding that poor job security and mortgages based on two salaries make it possible for anyone to fall into financial problems with sudden loss of work, Unafund seeks to enable people to keep their home and self-esteem.

HOW IT WORKS

Working on referrals from any organisation supplying free money/housing advice, Unafund awards interest-free loans in the form of a cheque made out to the mortgage lender or landlord. Repayment begins at an affordable amount on a weekly or monthly basis. The peace of mind offered by an interest-free loan allows the client to attend job interviews without a look of desperation and worry, greatly increasing their chances of finding new employment.

DEVELOPMENT

Unafund is built on a very simple idea. Its development is obviously related to generating a larger income in order to be able to grant more loans. In addition to this growth, there are plans to set up a monthly newsletter keeping subscribing members up to date on the work their giving allows.

THINGS TO CONSIDER

- An initiative such as this requires certain skills (financial, administrative, legal). Does your church have contact with people with the knowledge to tackle a demanding project?
- Does your church have the capital to set up a project like Unafund?

- If you don't have a financial pool from which you could make interest-free (or low-interest) loans, how could you raise money for this?
- If your church is unable to create a project working in this area, could you commit to supporting existing projects like Unafund?

HOW TO GET FUNDING

Unafund has limited running costs as it has no employees, and it is funded entirely by donations. Members pay a monthly subscription to support the project's work. Additional revenue is received by one-off donations and fund-raising events.

FOR ADVICE AND MORE INFORMATION CONTACT:

Alan Evans,
Unafund,
66 Liverpool Road South,
Burscough,
Ormskirk,
Lancashire,
L40 7TA
Tel: 01704 892197
Email: admin@una-support.co.uk
Web: www.una-fund.co.uk

'To extend our ability to prevent homelessness, the trustees recently decided to offer loans to people suddenly made homeless with insufficient money to pay the deposit to rent a suitable property. We look forward to experiencing the joy of helping more people to enjoy a settled home life.'

57. The Community Debt Advice Centre

Debt is endemic in our society. We live in an age in which owing huge sums of money is not only commonplace, it is the norm. It is alarmingly easy for the debts we take for granted to get out of hand. The Community Debt Advice Centre exists to help people from the Burgess Hill area manage their debts.

HOW IT WORKS

Debt is a difficult problem. It carries with it intense feelings of guilt, shame and often fear. It seems that there is no escape. The Community Debt Advice Centre addresses all of these problems by listening and offering advice to its clients, but also negotiating achievable payment structures with creditors. The centre offers its service free, as it recognises that the last thing people with financial difficulties need is a further fee to pay. This means that the staff are free to spend as much time with each client as they need, as there is no profit margin to consider. Essentially the project is about investing time in people to enable them to sort out their problems.

DEVELOPMENT

The Community Debt Advice Centre is constantly meeting new clients and working on their behalf, encouraging and helping them to clear their debts in a manageable way.

THINGS TO CONSIDER

- What provision is there for those struggling with debt in your area?
- Of these services, how many operate on a non-profit-making basis?
- Could your church offer a debt counselling service?

- Could you work in partnership with the local Citizens Advice Bureau?

HOW TO GET FUNDING

The Community Debt Advice Centre has limited running costs as it has no salaried staff. The project is funded by Burgess Hill Community Church, who supply an annual budget as well as its premises. Occasional one-off gifts also help fund the project.

FOR ADVICE AND MORE INFORMATION CONTACT:

The Community Debt Advice Centre,
12 Mill Road,
Burgess Hill,
West Sussex,
RH15 8DR
Tel: 01444 232444
Email: enquiries@debtadvicecentre.com
Web: www.debtadvicecentre.com

To read more about the Community Debt Advice Centre see *Faithworks: Stories of Hope.*

'Every one of our advisors would say that once you get into debt advice you cannot stop. To see the change in people's lives is so rewarding. My vision is that every single church in the UK would have at least one person trained in debt advice.'

58. The Stopsley Project – Food Pantry

A partnership between Stopsley Baptist Church and Spurgeon's Childcare, the Stopsley Project has been working in Luton for the last 15 years. The project aims to support families within the local community through a variety of initiatives. Focusing on family issues, principally parenting, the project seeks to enhance and enable stable family life.

HOW IT WORKS

The Stopsley Project Food Pantry offers practical help to struggling families. A store of tinned and dried foods, gathered from the harvest collections of local schools and churches, is held and distributed to families in need. The Food Pantry is principally offered to families with whom the Stopsley Project works. However, Social Services also have access to the store and pay for the food it takes for distribution. Families can phone the project when they cannot provide food for themselves or when they do not have enough money to pay the bills. Although the Stopsley Project rarely gives people money, by providing food, money is freed up for bill payment or essential purchases.

DEVELOPMENT

The Stopsley Project Food Pantry will not only continue to be an ongoing service to the local community, but increasingly look for ways of integrating the help it offers with other services.

THINGS TO CONSIDER

- Could your church keep supplies of non-perishable food items to distribute to those in need?

- Could you work in partnership with Social Services?
- How might you go about collecting the food?
- Could you supply other goods as well?

HOW TO GET FUNDING

The Stopsley Project Food Pantry has limited running costs as the food is provided through community donations and volunteers undertake the majority of the operational output. Any funding required is provided by Stopsley Baptist Church and voluntary gifts.

FOR ADVICE AND MORE INFORMATION CONTACT:

The Stopsley Project,
Stopsley Baptist Church,
St Thomas' Road,
Luton,
Bedfordshire,
LU2 7XP
Tel: 01582 405293
Fax: 01582 418357
Email: office@stopsley.net
Web: www.stopsley.net

'Then the righteous will answer him , "Lord, when did we see you hungry and feed you, or thirsty and give you something to drink?" . . . The King will reply, "I tell you the truth, whatever you did for the least of these brothers of mine, you did for me."' (Matthew 25:37–40.)

59. The Besom

The Besom Foundation provides a bridge between those who want to give and those who are in need. Instead of focusing solely on those in need, The Besom works hard to connect the two.

HOW IT WORKS

Set up in 1987, The Besom Foundation helps people make a difference. It provides opportunities for those who want to give time, skills, money or other resources to impact the lives of those in need. The Besom arranges projects across inner London enabling church-based groups, families and individuals to help people who are unable to help themselves. This might be in giving time to garden, tidy or paint someone's house; in donating goods which The Besom passes on to those who need them; or in giving money which is allocated to different projects by the giver, in the UK or overseas.

DEVELOPMENT

The Besom Foundation's development is limited only by the number of people involved. Besom is keen to grow across the country and offers a start-up pack for those who want to replicate the project, BIAS (Besom In A Suitcase).

THINGS TO CONSIDER

- Could your church start up a Besom project?
- Can you think of a better way to put those who want to give in touch with those who need to receive?
- Could you work with the other churches in your area to co-ordinate a joint project?

HOW TO GET FUNDING

All of the money gathered by The Besom is given to charities and projects. Its ongoing running costs are provided by individual gifts, specifically given for that purpose.

FOR ADVICE AND MORE INFORMATION CONTACT:

The Besom,
Tel: 020 7223 6544
Fax: 020 7223 6548
Email: besom@ukgateway.net

'Like most people we have things at home that we do not use, so The Besom was brilliant for us – it felt so good to give away some furniture and clothing and know they would go to families who really need them. It was easy too as The Besom collected everything from us.'

60. Newport North West Credit Union

NNWCU started in 1997 on the Bettws Estate. Its beginnings emanated from the concern of local Christians over the activities of loan sharks on the estate. A group from three local churches (URC, Anglican and Catholic) organised a series of open meetings, following which the project was launched.

HOW IT WORKS

The NNWCU exists simply to help relieve the financial difficulties of the people of Bettws. It now has over 420 members. Though it has one paid development worker, volunteers (who are members of the credit union) carry out most of the work. Apart from its base in the main shopping centre of the estate it also has weekly collection points at the local Catholic and Baptist churches and the community hall. All the local churches are represented on the management board. The NNWCU is a great example of churches working together to combat financial exclusion and promote bonding within the community.

DEVELOPMENT

The original plan of the NNWCU was to help the people of the Bettws estate – a highly deprived community. However, it was soon decided to extend the project, reaching out to other estates in the area.

THINGS TO CONSIDER

- Is debt a problem in your area?
- Are loan sharks operating, compounding the problems of already struggling people?
- Are there any other projects like NNWCU working in your area?

- If there are, are they fully meeting the needs of your community or is there still an unmet demand?

HOW TO GET FUNDING

For full funding details contact Caritas Social Action for their Grow Your Own Guide to Credit Unions. This tells you all about the history, growth and purpose of credit unions. It gives advice on how to set one up in your local area, the legal requirements and how to fund them.

FOR ADVICE AND MORE INFORMATION CONTACT:

Caritas Social Action,
39 Eccleston Square,
London,
SW1V 1BX
Tel: 020 7901 4875
Web: www.caritas-socialaction.org.uk

'We were drowning in debt, my husband had lost his job and it seemed like there was no way out . . . the credit union really helped us out. I don't know what would have happened without them.'

61. TELCO – The Living Wage

The East London Communities Organisation (TELCO) was launched on 20 November 1996. TELCO is an alliance of local churches, mosques, community groups, school communities and other associations committed to working together for the common good across four boroughs in East London.

HOW IT WORKS

One of TELCO's most important campaigns is for a Living Wage. In many instances permanent jobs have been replaced by temporary contracts earning nothing more than the minimum wage. TELCO's aim is to persuade all the major public sector organisations in East London to oblige all contractors to pay at least the 'East London Living Wage'. An exact figure was agreed at TELCO's assembly in April 2001 as a result of detailed research into the needs of families in the area. The campaign is bringing TELCO member agencies into a working relationship with trade unions in East London who, on their own, have been unable to halt a process of falling and stagnating wages for many people who deliver public services.

DEVELOPMENT

TELCO hopes to continue its work ensuring that no one in East London is paid less than the living wage.

THINGS TO CONSIDER

- Could you work in partnership with other voluntary sector and faith communities to help the people of your area?
- What are the priority needs of your area?
- What goals would you set and how would you measure your achievement?

HOW TO GET FUNDING

Each community group pays an annual fee which is matched by funds from national denominations and foundations. The money pays for regular training opportunities, development of the membership and the salary of the organisers.

FOR ADVICE AND MORE INFORMATION CONTACT:

TELCO,
Catherine Howarth,
3 Merchant Street,
London,
E3 4UJ
Tel: 020 8983 9808

'As the statutory principal aims of the GLA include the promotion of economic development, wealth creation and social development, I am keen not to see any developments in public authority service delivery which are based on financial disadvantage for affected workers and their families.' (Ken Livingstone, Mayor of London)

62. Trussel Trust – The Food Bank

Set up by the Trussell Trust in December 2000, the Food Bank is a response to a need in the Salisbury area. The project simply collects and distributes food to those in need. In 2001 the Food Bank handled 8.8 tonnes of food, giving away the equivalent of 14,124 meals to individuals or families in crisis and local institutions.

HOW IT WORKS

Food is collected both from people shopping at supermarkets and from donations made through churches, schools and other groups. All of the food is then given out either in the form of 'emergency boxes' in rural areas, or through a voucher system at the Food Bank centre. The centre came about as a result of demand from local health professionals. It offers not only food, but also internet access, advocacy, debt counselling and a Citizens Advice Bureau. The Food Bank's clients are referred by care professionals and given a voucher to exchange for food. The project aims to supply the short-term needs of those in crisis. However, in some cases food has been provided over longer periods to enable the client to clear debts.

DEVELOPMENT

The Trussell Trust sees the Food Bank as a project which could be easily replicated across the country.

THINGS TO CONSIDER

- Is emergency provision for those in crisis offered by another agency in your area?
- Could your church work in partnership with the Trussell Trust in setting up a Food Bank in your area?

- What facilities and staff would you need to make the project work?

HOW TO GET FUNDING

The Food Bank has received funding from a variety of sources. Funds to cover start-up costs and ongoing expenses have been received from a variety of charitable trusts. Additionally the local authority has given some funding in the form of a community grant. Donations from individuals are also a significant source of income.

FOR ADVICE AND MORE INFORMATION CONTACT:

Trussell Trust,
25 Middleton Road,
Salisbury,
Wiltshire,
SP2 7AY

Tel/Fax: 01722 411244
Email: info@trusselltrust.org
Web: www.trusselltrust.org

'A child was sent home from school because he smelt; his mother, struggling to hold the family together, had no money for washing materials. These items were provided from the Food Bank, together with emergency food.'

63. The Speakeasy, Cardiff

We live in an age in which debt is commonplace – the average student will graduate with debts of around £15,000. The Speakeasy has been in operation for ten years offering advice and legal assistance to its clients. Seeing around 700 people a year, the qualified solicitors of the Speakeasy represent those who would otherwise not be represented.

HOW IT WORKS

The Speakeasy aims to provide legal services free of charge – representing its clients in the areas of debt, welfare benefits and housing – whether or not they qualify for legal aid. It frequently represents them in court – all free of charge. Simply by sharing their financial problems with the staff of volunteers and solicitors, clients are able to take the first steps towards managing their debt and in so doing free themselves from the pressures which can lead to depression, mental breakdown and sometimes suicide.

DEVELOPMENT

The long-term vision of the Speakeasy is to widen its reach. Currently it works mainly in Cardiff city centre; however, a new office has been opened on the poorer outskirts of the city. Ultimately it is hoped that the service can extend beyond South Wales.

THINGS TO CONSIDER

- A project like the Speakeasy requires qualified solicitors. Does your church have anyone with the necessary skills to work in this area?
- Could you work in partnership with local solicitors, funding their work when Legal Aid does not?

HOW TO GET FUNDING

For funding, the centre relies on gifts from individuals and churches. Additionally, it receives some funding from grant-making bodies and from its own fundraising activities. Council funding was agreed for the first time this year. Also some revenue comes from the Legal Services Commission in the form of Legal Aid.

> FOR ADVICE AND MORE INFORMATION CONTACT:
>
> The Speakeasy Advice Centre,
> 2 Arabella Street,
> Roath,
> Cardiff,
> CF24 4TA
> Tel: 029 2045 3111
> Fax: 029 2045 1064
> Email: s.ac@speakeasyadvice.co.uk

'Without the Speakeasy I couldn't have managed. Having the caseworker help me with everything took all the stress off me. I can't thank [them] enough.'

SECTION 8:

Housing

64. Huntingdonshire Housing Partnership Limited

The Huntingdonshire Housing Partnership Limited (HHP) was formed to buy nearly 7,000 council properties, and has become the region's premier landlord, with 9,000 tenants and providing homes for between 25–30,000 people. The cost of the purchase was almost £65m, which released massive cash reserves to the local authority to develop local services – this was a deal with many winners!

HOW IT WORKS

HHP is a 'social landlord', bound by government regulations and is non-profit-making. It has a £20 million turnover, a £95m loan facility, the opportunity to build new homes, and 250 employees. Through careful planning the company is able to guarantee that, for the foreseeable future, rents will not rise by more than one per cent above inflation and that major home improvements and good local services will be provided. HHP has also introduced initiatives to help make communities safer, with neighbourhood and street wardens who deal with problems such as graffiti and litter, acting as a source of mediation between neighbours and a contact for the isolated.

DEVELOPMENT

HHP is now seeking to develop the LUMINUS Group, consisting of three new companies including a charity (to maximise tax efficiency), to share its distinctive ethos more widely and to expand regionally and nationally.

THINGS TO CONSIDER

- Could the churches of your area realistically launch a project of this size?
- If not, what ideas does it give you about what might be more achievable?
- How might your church work in partnership with other organisations on a housing project?

HOW TO GET FUNDING

HHP has borrowed substantial funds from financial institutions. They are, however, moving towards financial self-sufficiency – the majority of their funding now coming from rent.

FOR ADVICE AND MORE INFORMATION CONTACT:

Chan Abraham – Chief Executive,
Huntingdonshire Housing Partnership,
Brook House,
Ouse Walk,
Huntingdon,
PE29 3QW
Tel: 01480 396701
Email: info@hhp.org.uk
Web: www.hhp.org.uk

'We have to balance an appropriately commercial approach with being socially responsible. At our core we are meeting the needs of some of the most vulnerable people in our communities. We want to achieve this through really good strategic planning and resource management.'

65. Banbury Homes – Tenancy Support Service

In times of crisis many people find that they are unable to cope financially and are in danger of losing their tenancy as a result. With the death of a close relative, unemployment, debt or a drug- or alcohol- dependent spouse, it becomes difficult to pay the bills and maintain a tenancy. In such situations the Tenancy Support Service can help.

HOW IT WORKS

Opened in October 2001, the North Oxfordshire Tenancy Support Service offers help to those people who are in temporary difficulties which might affect their tenancy. The project deals with around 150 clients at any one time. With such a wide client base the four support workers encounter an enormous variety of needs. Where possible these needs are dealt with directly by the project; however, a major part of its work is in connecting its clients with the appropriate agencies to help them. BTSS works with its clients over an average period of around six months, helping them to get back on their feet and maintain their tenancy independently.

DEVELOPMENT

The Tenancy Support Service intends to further develop its high standards of working practice. It sees the training and development of its staff as a key to this goal. It also aims to enhance its links with the statutory support services.

THINGS TO CONSIDER

- What financial needs are present in your community? How have you assessed these?

- What can your church do to meet those needs?
- Would a project like the Tenancy Support Service benefit the people of your community?

HOW TO GET FUNDING

The Tenancy Support Service receives funding from the Supporting People fund. Further to this, it has been considerably resourced by the local church, which has invested time and prayer as well as money in its development.

> FOR ADVICE AND MORE INFORMATION CONTACT:
>
> North Oxfordshire Tenancy Support Service,
> Banbury Homes Ltd,
> 58 George Street,
> Banbury,
> OX16 5BH
> Tel: 01295 265439
> Email: DRG@banburyhomes.org.uk

'It's great to have someone to talk to . . . someone who can help you when you've got yourself in a bit of a mess . . . there are so many things to handle and sometimes they just all pile up on top of you and you can't see a way out.'

66. Shaftesbury Housing Group – Kingsmead Homes

The Kingsmead estate is a well-known area of deprivation within the London Borough of Hackney. The estate consists of 16 medium-rise blocks of flats connected by long balconies. A total of 981 dwellings house an estimated population of some 2,300 people from a wide variety of ethnic backgrounds.

HOW IT WORKS

Elsewhere we have looked at the work that the Hackney Marsh Partnership set up to support the residents of Kingsmead in a variety of ways. However, the Shaftesbury Housing Group's Kingsmead Homes is working at a complementary level looking at the physical environment of the estate. Aside from minor repairs to the central heating in the 1980s, the flats have not been touched since they were built in the 1930s. Kingsmead Homes is undertaking the massive work of the modernisation of the housing on the estate, the aim being to improve the quality of life, to re-utilise what has been unwanted housing, and, through the increase in morale and pride on the estate, to reduce crime levels.

DEVELOPMENT

The planning is ongoing – the building work will not be finished until late 2003.

THINGS TO CONSIDER

- Is there a housing estate in your community which needs radical physical regeneration?
- Would your local council be open to working with an agency such as the Shaftesbury Housing Group?
- What could your church do to help?

HOW TO GET FUNDING

Kingsmead Homes has received a dowry from central government of £9.5 million, a Single Regeneration Budget grant from the council of £3.5 million and loans from Dexia Municipal Bank.

FOR ADVICE AND MORE INFORMATION CONTACT:

Nigel J. G. Poole,
Chief Executive,
9a Kingsmead Way,
Hackney,
London,
E9 5QG
Tel: 020 8525 9876
Fax: 020 8525 9452
Email: njp@kingsmeadhomes.org.uk
Web: www.kingsmeadhomes.org.uk

'Kingsmead Homes aims to work with the community to improve lives and lifestyles providing better homes at affordable rents, along with a better living environment and economic opportunities for tenants of the estate.' (Mission Statement)

67. Banbury Homes – Cotefield House

Opened in May 2000 to provide housing with support for ten homeless families, Cotefield House is a large Victorian property on the edge of Banbury. The project aims to house families who would otherwise be forced to live in bed and breakfast accommodation, offering a more secure solution to temporary housing difficulties.

HOW IT WORKS

Families are referred to Cotefield House by the local council. Tenants usually arrive at Cotefield House in a state of crisis, struggling with problems that have precipitated their homelessness. The aim is to address any issues faced by the residents with the support of staff and other supporting agencies, enabling them to regain independence in their housing as quickly as possible. To date, over 40 families have benefited from the fully furnished flats in the house. Of these only seven families have not gone on to permanent housing.

DEVELOPMENT

Cotefield House aims to do more than 'fire-fight', seeing the prevention of homelessness through community education as of equal importance to supporting those in crisis. It is also working to further develop its links with local statutory support services.

THINGS TO CONSIDER

- What facilities are there for homeless families in your area?
- Does your church have a building which could be used in a similar way to Cotefield House?

- If not, how might you access the facilities you would need to set up a project like this?

HOW TO GET FUNDING

Cotefield House is funded both through rent paid by its residents as well as grants from the Supporting People fund. Additional support has been received from the local church.

FOR ADVICE AND MORE INFORMATION CONTACT:

Cotefield House,
Banbury Homes Ltd,
58 George Street,
Banbury,
OX16 5BH
Tel: 01295 265439
Email: DRG@banburyhomes.org.uk

'[Our duty is] to succour the orphans and widows, and those who through sickness or any other cause are in want, and those who are in bonds, and the strangers sojourning amongst us.' (Justin Martyr – third-century church leader)

68. Ashley Homes – Coopers Court

For many people, old age is a time of great difficulty, dealing with feelings of loneliness, isolation and a loss of independence. For many elderly people, as they become less able to look after themselves, registered care accommodation is often the only option. Coopers Court, however, exists as an alternative to registered care.

HOW IT WORKS

A product of a partnership between the Shaftesbury Housing Group, the London Borough of Tower Hamlets and the Coopers Livery Company, Coopers Court is a new development of flats for the elderly. The aim of the project is to allow residents to continue living independently (or to return to independence after a stay in care accommodation) while having the level of help on hand appropriate to each individual. Tenants receive personal care and support from Ashley Homes staff who are based on site, work in partnership with locally based community health care professionals, and operate a Key Worker system that ensures continuity of care for all.

DEVELOPMENT

Coopers Court is constantly looking for ways to better serve its tenants, with individual support plans established to help each resident regain their independence and dignity.

THINGS TO CONSIDER

- What provision is there to help elderly people in your area to retain appropriate independence?
- Could your church help older people to stay in their own homes?

- What systems would you need to put in place to ensure that older people in your community were regularly visited and cared for?

HOW TO GET FUNDING

The Coopers Court Development cost £7.2 million to design and build. This was funded in part by the Coopers Livery Company. In the future statutory funding will be sought from the Supporting People initiative.

FOR ADVICE AND MORE INFORMATION CONTACT:

Mary Harris,
Director of Supported Housing,
Ashley Homes,
Shaftesbury House,
87 East Street,
Epsom,
KT17 1DT
Tel: 01372 736823
Fax: 01372 736899
Email: ashelp@ashleyhomes.org.uk
Web: www.ashleyhomes.org.uk

'Ashley Homes' values reflect the Christian ethos of the Shaftesbury Housing Association, of which we are a part. Our residential homes are for people who, even with domiciliary support, are unable to live in their own home.'

SECTION 9:

Recycling, The Environment

69. The Wildwood Project

In response to the large-scale unemployment created by the closure of two local coal mines, the local church set up the Wildwood project. The project renovates old furniture and wood to create high quality products for the home and garden. At the same time Wildwood reclaims unemployed people by offering them real training for real jobs.

HOW IT WORKS

Wildwood not only operates as a self-sustaining furniture making and renovation project, but also functions as an 'intermediate labour market' – providing training to get people back to work and linking them with potential employers. Some 86 per cent of those who have passed through the project are now in permanent employment. It prides itself on taking a holistic and individually tailored approach to each of its trainees.

DEVELOPMENT

There are many plans for the future development of Wildwood, including the launch of a new initiative providing employment and training for adults with learning difficulties, focusing on the horticultural development of wasteland.

THINGS TO CONSIDER

- Does your church have (or could you obtain) premises which could be opened up to the unemployed?
- What skills would be necessary to launch a project similar to Wildwood?

HOW TO GET FUNDING

Wildwood has received Single Regeneration Budget money as well as European Social Funding and other grants. In addition, a great emphasis is placed on the revenue generated by the sales of the project's products.

FOR ADVICE AND MORE INFORMATION CONTACT:

Ann Menzies-Blythe,
The Wildwood Project Bentley Ltd,
The Training Centre,
High Street,
Bentley,
Doncaster,
DN5 0AA
Tel: 01302 822228
Email: ann@wildwoodcompany.fsnet.co.uk

'Training and mentoring support, along with key skills provision, help address the very real barriers faced by each person we work with. A third of our trainees have been unemployed for over three years – 17 years in one case.'

70. Second Thoughts Community Shop

Sutton Coldfield Baptist Church wanted to set up a community project to get the church out of its building and meet people with whom they may not normally come into contact. Staffed by local church members, Second Thoughts is a shop that serves the community both through the sale of second-hand goods and the reinvestment of profits in local projects.

HOW IT WORKS

A central aim of Second Thoughts is to build relationships within the community. To this end it serves tea and coffee free of charge, to encourage people to stop and chat, and over time many friendships have been established. Second Thoughts is more than a charity shop; it is a hub of community life, providing both material and spiritual support to its customers and drawing the church and community closer together. A demonstration of the project's investment in people is its practice of marking customers' birthdays and other special occasions with the giving of gifts.

DEVELOPMENT

Second Thoughts currently offers its customers information on services and facilities in the local area. It is hoped that in the future this role might be expanded, making the shop a comprehensive 'one-stop' information centre with internet access and packs detailing local resources.

THINGS TO CONSIDER

- What social and spiritual needs in your community are not currently being met?
- Could opening a shop like Second Thoughts help to meet those needs?

- Do you, as a church, have the skills to plan and set up this kind of project?

HOW TO GET FUNDING

Second Thoughts is largely self-funded but does receive some top-up funding from the church, which contributes to the salary of the project coordinator. The shop is staffed by volunteers.

FOR ADVICE AND MORE INFORMATION CONTACT:

Second Thoughts,
23 Churchill Parade,
Falcon Lodge,
Sutton Coldfield,
West Midlands,
B75 7LD
Tel: 0121 311 2892
Email: georgie@suttoncoldfieldbaptistchurch.org.uk

'We believe that God loves us because of who we are and not in spite of who we are. We believe that God wants us to show people that God loves them and wants the best for them.'

71. Mustard Tree, Manchester

Originally launched in 1993 as a project for Manchester's homeless population, Mustard Tree has grown and developed its work. It offers a range of services supporting people with a wide range of needs relating to accommodation, including a furniture recycling project. The service is open to anyone in need and is now working extensively with asylum seekers.

HOW IT WORKS

Mustard Tree holds a wide range of household goods, clothing, electrical items, furniture and even toys, which are usually donated by local churches. Clients visit the centre (usually by appointment) where they are able to obtain the things they need free of charge, or, in the case of non-essential items and electrical goods, for a modest price. The project also offers training initiatives by providing weekly courses in IT skills, English as a second language, and a furniture restoration workshop.

DEVELOPMENT

In the future, Mustard Tree aims to increase the size of its furniture store, increasing the number of clients it can serve. The launch of a charity shop is also being considered to generate revenue through the sale of surplus stock.

THINGS TO CONSIDER

- Is there an unmet need for a project like Mustard Tree in your area?
- If you were to run a furniture recycling project, where would you store your stock?
- Would your project need full-time staff, or could it be staffed on a voluntary basis?

- From what sources would you gather goods to distribute?

HOW TO GET FUNDING

Mustard Tree receives financial support from the European Social Fund, grant-making trusts, individual supporters and local churches. Additional revenue is gained by the sale of goods.

FOR ADVICE AND MORE INFORMATION CONTACT:

Dave Smith,
Unity House,
42 Great Southern Street,
Rusholme,
Manchester,
M14 4EZ
Tel: 0161 256 1331
Email: mustard.tree@bigfoot.com
Web: www.mustardtree.co.uk

'In 1999 Dave Smith visited my church and gave a presentation about the Mustard Tree. I was keen to volunteer my services and have been involved ever since. I really enjoy the street work and God has blessed me in a variety of ways as a result.'

72. UK Reclaim

UK Reclaim was launched in June 2001 as a facilitating body helping to launch new enterprises and initiatives in the social sector. The first of these projects is in Reading and aims to provide jobs for the unemployed, at the same time as tackling the environmental issue of waste.

HOW IT WORKS

Essentially UK Reclaim, Reading, operates on two levels. First the reclamation and re-use of wood that would otherwise go into landfill sites. The project is gearing up to be able to receive around 500 tonnes of wood waste a month, which it sorts, grades and returns to either product manufacturing workshops, the DIY market or for use as chipboard. Second, the provision of paid employment to people who might otherwise be socially excluded – in effect helping to rebuild people. The social and environmental benefits of this project are clear. However, beyond that, it is hoped that UK Reclaim will be a vehicle through which the church can be recognised by corporate and local government as a relevant player in the realisation of sustainable community development.

DEVELOPMENT

UK Reclaim plans to extend beyond Reading, starting similar enterprises across the UK.

THINGS TO CONSIDER

- Does your theology of creation impact the way you view recycling?
- What steps can your church take towards reclamation, re-use and recycling?

- How might you involve others in these ideas, benefiting the wider community as well as the environment?

HOW TO GET FUNDING

UK Reclaim has received 'pump priming' funding from private trusts as well as interest-free loans from supporters. However, within two years it is planned that UK Reclaim will be self-funding and will have surplus funds to invest in other initiatives.

FOR ADVICE AND MORE INFORMATION CONTACT:

Nick Crowder, CEO,
UK Reclaim,
Lane End Farm,
Shinfield Road,
Reading,
Berkshire,
RG2 9BE
Tel: 0118 988 5900.
Email: nick@ukreclaim.co.uk

'UK Reclaim is: developing God-given talents, reclaiming natural resources, building community from the ground up.'

73. The Sutton Furniture Project

The Sutton Furniture Project provides top condition second-hand furniture and other household goods to those in the local community who are in need. A bi-product is the provision of job skills experience for people who are unemployed, including basic furniture restoration, van driving, warehouse and office training.

HOW IT WORKS

Clients, referred by over 40 local agencies, are provided with high quality furniture and service. The project aims to demonstrate a true interest in the people it serves, reflecting the love of Christ to the community, not just through a response to physical need but also through the relationships that are built. A further aim is to provide an environment conducive to building confidence and skills in those who volunteer with the project, which increasingly includes those from beyond the church.

DEVELOPMENT

The provision of furniture and household goods is only the beginning – a sticking plaster. The Sutton Furniture Project is keen to provide a more holistic service for the community – for instance, increasing training and job skills opportunities, offering support with budgeting and other life skills, as well as helping to renovate run-down housing.

HOW TO GET FUNDING

At present the Sutton Furniture Project is funded entirely by grants, client donations and individual donations from supporters. Funding is currently being sought for staff and buildings to advance the work of the project.

THINGS TO CONSIDER

- Is there a demand for a furniture project in your area?
- A project of this nature is extremely labour-intensive – will you have enough volunteers to make the project work?
- What partnerships could you form locally in order to set up a similar project?

FOR ADVICE AND MORE INFORMATION CONTACT:

The Sutton Furniture Project,
Vineyard House,
4 Greenford Road,
Sutton,
Surrey,
SM1 1JY
Tel: 020 8642 7766
Email: sfp@vineyardchurch.org

'You can think of Vineyard Church as a group of people "doing life together". We are a faith community on a journey, people with a shared mission.'

SECTION 10:

Community

74. Christian Community Action Ministries

Evolving from a derelict barn and one person's vision ten years ago, CCA is now Reading's leading social support agency with six high street based, self-financing, Community Support Centres resourced through a central administrative service and a 17,000 sq. ft. materials warehouse. These facilities enable the local church to meet the needs of hundreds of local people every month.

HOW IT WORKS

CCA aims to support and facilitate the work of the local church. Through its Community Support Centres, CCA distributes clothes, food, furnishings, bedding and appliances to those in the community in great need. These goods are collected from the community both through a chain of charity shops which retail surplus stock, and their central clearing centre. The project receives around 1500 tonnes of goods a year. Clearly such a project creates a huge amount of work and through this CCA is able to offer rehabilitation and work training to those wishing to break from benefit dependency and unemployment.

DEVELOPMENT

CCA aims to replicate these highly successful social enterprises and social outreaches across the country. Their goal is to empower Christians and demonstrate that the church is relevant to the needs of people today.

THINGS TO CONSIDER

- What could you do to enable other churches in your area to meet the needs of your community?

- How might you work together with other groups to achieve more?
- Would a project like CCA benefit your community or are needs currently being met by an existing agency?

HOW TO GET FUNDING

Initially CCA received most of its funding from Christian trusts and individual donations. However, over the last six years it has developed to a point where it is around 75 per cent self-funded and sustainable.

FOR ADVICE AND MORE INFORMATION CONTACT:

Nick Crowder,
Christian Community Action,
369 Oxford Road,
Reading,
Berkshire,
RG30 1HA
Tel: 0118 951 2336
Email: nick@ccam.org.uk

'God said CCA was to be a gift to the church and not a burden. Therefore we do not seek financial support. We believe we are to be a beacon of faith and trust in God's provision for all that we do and plan in the future.'

75. Maybridge – Community-LINK

Community-LINK is a good neighbour scheme which links volunteers to local residents who request help. Though time is limited, help is offered for free and covers a variety of tasks including gardening, shopping, housework, transport and advocacy.

HOW IT WORKS

The voluntary opportunities available are wide-ranging and constantly being redefined by the changing needs of the residents. Community-LINK volunteers work directly with residents, as well as alongside various voluntary and statutory organisations. Some users of the scheme have been referred to Community-LINK from statutory agencies. Essentially the project reduces the risk of vulnerable adults losing their independence by providing free, low-level, practical intervention and through facilitating neighbourliness by encouraging people to help one another.

DEVELOPMENT

It is hoped that, over time, Community-LINK will help to develop true community – in which people will naturally help each other without the need for outside intervention.

THINGS TO CONSIDER

- What tasks could volunteers from your church undertake in local homes?
- What are the risks that are involved for volunteers in this kind of project?
- What are the training and support needs for volunteers?
- Do you have insurance for personal and public liability?

HOW TO GET FUNDING

Community-LINK has been funded chiefly by the Maybridge Community Church 'community budget'. However, additional funds have been generated through donations from local residents.

FOR ADVICE AND MORE INFORMATION CONTACT:

The MILE Project,
c/o Maybridge Community Church,
The Strand,
Maybridge,
Worthing,
West Sussex,
BN12 6DL
Tel: 01903 603337
Email: info@mile-project.org.uk
Web: www.mile-project.org.uk

'Just to say thank you for giving me my dream garden, and for all your hard work and time. Thank you to everyone for making it possible.'

76. Buttershaw Christian Family Centre

Based at the local Baptist church, the Buttershaw Christian Family Centre grew out of a desire to engage with the community of the Buttershaw Estate, Bradford. Over its eleven-year life, the centre has expanded from its original work of an employment scheme to offer a wide range of services.

HOW IT WORKS

The overall aim of the project is to show 'God's love in action on the Buttershaw Estate'. The emphasis of the centre has developed from the days of the original employment scheme to cover two principal areas – supporting parents and building community. The Buttershaw Christian Family Centre seeks to include the excluded. Parenting activities include a playgroup, young mums' group, 'learning to play' courses, music and dance clubs, craft activities and literacy groups. Community-building initiatives include a credit union, 'Sizzles' breakfast bar, 'The Meeting Place' family lunchtime, and a planned internet connected community café.

DEVELOPMENT

The Buttershaw Christian Family Centre is constantly expanding and the purchase of a new building is planned to facilitate this growth. The centre is working with a variety of local bodies, including the local Community Regeneration Board and the local Anglican and Methodist churches.

THINGS TO CONSIDER

- Does your neighbourhood include any large housing estates in which social and spiritual need is likely to be great?
- How might you integrate your church into that community

and the community into your church?
- What specific areas of need could you address?
- How will you ensure that you don't force middle-class values onto others?

HOW TO GET FUNDING

The Buttershaw Christian Family Centre receives financial support from a number of sources, including Children in Need, Spurgeon's Childcare, Bradford Metropolitan Council and various other grant-making trusts.

FOR ADVICE AND MORE INFORMATION CONTACT:

The Revd Stuart Gregg,
Buttershaw Christian Family Centre,
The Crescent,
Bradford,
BD6 3PZ
Tel: 01274 690262
Email: stuart.gregg@buttershawbaptist.org.uk
Web: www.buttershawbaptist.org.uk

'. . . there is still much work to do. We've not run out of vision. We look forward to the future at Buttershaw as we work together building a family centre that is at the heart of the community.'

77. Mornington Community Project

The Mornington Community Project has been working for the 'holistic well-being' of the Lower Ormeau Road area of Belfast for over 12 years. Initiated by local women in 1989, the focus of the project has been on finding positive and practical answers to socio-economic disadvantage and the vicious sectarian strife that has threatened to destroy the community.

HOW IT WORKS

The Lower Ormeau Road area of Belfast is a place of great need – unemployment of 18–25-year-olds stands at 65 per cent and the toll taken by the issues surrounding sectarian division is high. The Mornington Project currently operates an advice centre, a coffee shop, several different youth clubs, a women's group, a mother and toddler group, a homework club, a senior citizens' group and employment training. These initiatives bring not only relief to immediate physical needs but also reconciliation. The project is a place where all are welcome and in which former enemies can work together for the good of the community.

DEVELOPMENT

The Mornington Community Project is keen to share its vision to help others develop similar community-building initiatives.

THINGS TO CONSIDER

- The Mornington Project works in a divided community. Are there any signs of division in your community?
- What could be done to unite divided parties?
- How do you see your church fitting into that work?
- What practical needs must be met along the way?

HOW TO GET FUNDING

The Mornington Community Project is funded by grant-making trusts, individual donations and, to a limited degree, funding from statutory agencies.

FOR ADVICE AND MORE INFORMATION CONTACT:

Ken Humphries,
The Mornington Community Project,
117 Ormeau Road,
Belfast,
B17 1SH
Tel: 028 9033 0911
Fax: 028 9024 2730
Email: info@mornington-belfast.org
Web: www.mornington-belfast.org

'What enables us? Above all, in all, through all, in spite of everything – God! If you are on speaking terms with him, please pray for Lower Ormeau – at least once a week or every day if you can.'

78. Avencare – Advocacy and Befriending Service

The Avencare project in Preston, Lancashire, provides social support to local people while at the same time building and developing a sense of community. Avencare was originally initiated in 1997 by Catholic Caring Services as part of their community development programme. The project is now jointly run by a local Roman Catholic church and an Anglican church.

HOW IT WORKS

Avencare aims to provide social support within a community setting, regardless of whether or not clients belong to a faith group. It responds to need by developing self-help initiatives. Where possible, goals are fulfilled by training local volunteers to provide leadership, thus encouraging a greater sense of community cohesion and well-being. One of its initiatives, the Advocacy and Befriending Service, supports people between the ages of 25 and 55 who are struggling socially or financially. The service provides face-to-face home support by befriending, listening and giving advice and information. It aims to raise self-confidence in the person and so help them to help themselves.

DEVELOPMENT

The Advocacy and Befriending Service aims to enhance its relationships with other organisations, especially local social, health, housing, and drug/alcohol services, to enable its work to develop.

THINGS TO CONSIDER

- How might your church support people with social support needs in your area?
- Is home visiting something that your church could undertake?
- Who in your church would staff a project such as this?
- Would you need to employ a full-time project coordinator?

HOW TO GET FUNDING

Avencare has received the majority of its funding from charitable trusts, some of which have contributed significant start-up grants, while others have offered funding on a more limited scale.

FOR ADVICE AND MORE INFORMATION CONTACT:

Joseph Cobb,
Avencare,
c/o The Foxton Centre,
Knowsley Street,
Preston,
Lancashire,
PR1 3SA
Tel: 01772 558404

'Avencare aims to work within the local community alongside individuals and groups with an interest in the area, including those involved in other local initiatives.'

79. The Thornbury Centre

Thornbury is a suburb of Bradford which suffers from high levels of poverty, lack of community and rising crime fuelled by drug abuse, which is endemic. Out of this climate came a church that decided not to meet in a traditional building but rather to develop a centre designed to serve the community.

HOW IT WORKS

The new church building 'The Thornbury Centre' was designed specifically to be open and relevant to the whole community. A range of programmes is operated from the centre, including an arts project which has commissioned public art and sculptures for some local housing estates (a simple measure which increases a sense of community), a lunch club, a café, the local library and various training courses operated by Bradford College. The centre, which now has 15 full-time staff and many more volunteers, has become the hub of the community in Thornbury.

DEVELOPMENT

The Thornbury Centre is constantly looking for ways to increase its service to the community.

THINGS TO CONSIDER

- How might your church buildings be better used for the good of the community?
- How could you help to re-establish a feeling of community in your area if it has been lost?
- How could you more accurately gauge the needs of your community?

HOW TO GET FUNDING

The Thornbury Centre has received funding from a number of different sources, including the Millennium Commission, the European Union and the local Regeneration Development Agency. Individual donations and tithes have also supported the project.

FOR ADVICE AND MORE INFORMATION CONTACT:

Paul Hackwood,
The Thornbury Centre,
Leeds Old Road,
Thornbury,
Bradford,
BD3 8JX
Tel: 01274 666649
Email: paulhackwood@aol.com

To read more about the Thornbury Centre, see *Faithworks: Stories of Hope.*

'Of course, all this is a journey. If we could have seen ten years ago what we are doing now, we would have been too afraid to begin. All we did back then was to take the one small step we could, and then another, and another – until we have reached the point where we are today.'

80. Maybridge – Community Teas

Maybridge Community Teas were set up to offer the elderly, vulnerable and those often confined to home an opportunity to get out and make new friends. Having grown out of a local survey, the Teas meet a recognised need in the community and have seen steadily increasing attendance. The Teas are enjoyable for guests and volunteers alike.

HOW IT WORKS

The Community Teas, which are run by Maybridge Community Church's 'MILE Project', provide a regular weekend social activity for older people, including quality entertainment within the financial reach of limited pension income. By providing entertainment (along with some tea and cake) the project helps relieve the burden of loneliness felt by many elderly people as it creates the environment to form friendships within the wider community. A further outcome is the greater integration of the church within the community, providing yet more opportunities for engagement with local residents.

DEVELOPMENT

The project aims to expand its service by offering regular outings for the elderly and isolated. The Community Teas will continue to grow as elderly people known to the church through other projects are invited to attend.

THINGS TO CONSIDER

- Is the social provision for the elderly or housebound within your community adequate?
- What gaps or weaknesses are there?
- How could your church fill these gaps?

HOW TO GET FUNDING

The Community Teas receive some funding from the West Sussex Social & Caring Services (Prevention Fund). This is supplemented by the Maybridge Community Church 'Community Budget'.

FOR ADVICE AND MORE INFORMATION CONTACT:

The MILE Project,
c/o Maybridge Community Church,
The Strand,
Maybridge,
Worthing,
West Sussex,
BN12 6DL
Tel: 01903 603337
Email: info@mile-project.org.uk
Web: www.mile-project.org.uk

'A wonderful and welcoming atmosphere. I wouldn't miss it for anything.'

81. The Eden Project, Manchester

Eden is a new style of youth project which brings life to some of the toughest areas of Manchester. Eden aims to see the inner-city communities of Manchester transformed by the power of God. This exciting vision was born over five years ago, with the first Eden being launched in 1997.

HOW IT WORKS

Originally launched in Wythenshawe as an initiative of The Message Trust, Eden aims to move up to 30 voluntary youth and community workers into each targeted region of Manchester to live on a long-term basis. These workers, in partnership with a local 'host' church, strive to see young people becoming Christians, discipled and integrated into a loving Christian community. The effects that Eden has on a community are palpable: crime is reduced and lives are changed. Through the building of real neighbourly relationships the projects have started to see communities changed.

DEVELOPMENT

The Eden project has developed buses which operate as part of its outreach programme and which also support its ongoing work in schools by providing support to PSE and RE departments.

THINGS TO CONSIDER

- What steps could you take to transform the rough communities of your area?
- Could people from your church move into these communities to live long term?
- How might your church have input into local schools?

- How could you avoid mistaking middle-class values for Christian values?

HOW TO GET FUNDING

Each new Eden project is funded by The Message Trust, which pays the full-time team during the early stages of its development. The host church is encouraged to give as much as possible to meet these ongoing costs. It is hoped that this giving will increase over time as the value of volunteer workers is realised by the host church.

FOR ADVICE AND MORE INFORMATION CONTACT:

Ruth Lacey,
Eden,
The Message,
P.O. Box 151,
Manchester
M22 4YY
Tel: 0161 946 2300
Fax: 0161 946 2310
Email: info@message.org.uk
Web: www.message.org.uk

'You have worked tremendously hard, with great creativity, to tackle some incredibly difficult social challenges. I am really impressed by what has been achieved through your efforts and confident that its positive impact will continue to grow.' (The Rt Hon. Iain Duncan Smith, MP)

82. Refugee Day Centre, West Croydon

The UK is home to a growing population of refugees and asylum seekers. These people are frequently marginalised within society, abused and the target of negative attitudes – not least from the tabloid press. The Refugee Day Centre aims to offer a welcoming atmosphere, as well as practical help and advice.

HOW IT WORKS

The Refugee Day Centre provides for the immediate needs of those it meets, offering clothing, toiletries, food parcels and household goods. But more than this, it also provides a place for refugees to meet and establish friendships – as well as a daily three-course meal. In addition, various educational courses teaching English and enabling whole families to learn together are available.

DEVELOPMENT

The Refugee Day Centre plans to expand its advice desk to include experts on housing, education, health and immigration. These services will further assist refugees and asylum seekers in adapting to life in Britain and making a contribution to the community.

THINGS TO CONSIDER

- Does your community have a large community of refugees?
- Are their needs being met by other organisations?
- What practical help could your church offer?

HOW TO GET FUNDING

The Refugee Day Centre is funded by Croydon Council and the Wates Foundation. Further funds are received through donations from churches and individuals.

FOR ADVICE AND MORE INFORMATION CONTACT:

Beryl Telman, Refugee Day Centre Coordinator,
Refugee Day Centre,
c/o West Croydon Baptist Church,
1 Whitehorse Road,
Croydon,
CRO 2JH
Tel: 020 8656 0696
Fax: 020 8684 2643
Email: refugeedaycentre@lineone.net

'We work hard to meet the specific needs of individuals, so we spend a great deal of time talking to each asylum seeker ascertaining how we can help that individual.'

83. The Furnival

The Furnival is a community project working in Burngreave – an area in Sheffield facing great deprivation. Only 9 per cent of the area's school leavers have five GCSEs at A–C grades (the national average is around 50 per cent), half of families are headed by a single parent, and the suicide rate is 60 per cent higher than the UK average.

HOW IT WORKS

Operating from an old pub building, The Furnival offers a variety of projects as a response to local social needs. For instance, the old pub cellar is used to help children who are at risk of exclusion from mainstream education, an art therapy room has been set up to help those suffering from mental illness to address some of the issues in their lives, and there is a growing work with asylum seekers. Working in an area of considerable deprivation is hard – something that The Furnival has felt. However, its commitment to transforming Burngreave is unchanged.

DEVELOPMENT

The Furnival was developed in response to the great needs of the community around it. It continues to change and develop to meet the changing demands of the people it serves.

THINGS TO CONSIDER

- What resources does your church have, however small they might seem?
- What realistic goals could you have in serving your community?
- How open are you to the reality that things might not work out as you expect?

HOW TO GET FUNDING

The Furnival has attracted funding from many sources, including the Single Regeneration Budget, the New Opportunities Fund, the Lotteries Board, Excellence in Cities, as well as from a range of charitable trusts and churches.

FOR ADVICE AND MORE INFORMATION CONTACT:

Jane Grinonneau,
The Furnival,
119 Verdon Street,
Sheffield
S3 9QQ
Tel: 01142 727497
Email: thefurnival@aol.com

'The members of The Furnival are Christians of several denominations who, by living out the way of Jesus, make real in the experience of the local community the loving presence of God.'

84. The High Impact Project

Father Jim Kennedy is the parish priest at the Church of the Blessed Sacrament, North London. His church is a hub for a plethora of community activities, a lot of which are run in partnership with other agencies. The parish is in the fourth most deprived local government ward in the country and encompasses 15 housing estates.

HOW IT WORKS

The Church of the Blessed Sacrament is engaged in a range of partnerships with organisations and statutory bodies committed to improving the environment for those living in the neighbourhood. It also helps to empower local people to participate in the changes going on around them. The High Impact Project was launched in March 2001. The church, the local council and a group of other voluntary sector organisations and housing associations formed a partnership to try to provide coordinated activities for young people in order to help them in the development of life skills. These include art, music, drama, sport and weekends away. The project's major focus is on young people otherwise excluded from school or wider society.

DEVELOPMENT

High Impact aims to open a Satellite Project on each of the local housing estates.

THINGS TO CONSIDER

- Could your church develop strategic relationships with other groups and statutory bodies to affect change in your community?

- What are the specific needs of your community which you could meet in partnership with other organisations?
- How might you remain distinctively Christian without alienating other groups?

HOW TO GET FUNDING

Funding for the High Impact Project comes mainly from the King's Cross Partnership. In a project which works in partnership with statutory bodies and other organisations, funding is not difficult to find.

FOR ADVICE AND MORE INFORMATION CONTACT:

Fr Jim Kennedy,
Church of the Blessed Sacrament,
Copenhagen Street,
London,
N1 0SR
Tel: 020 7837 4841
Web: www.caritas-socialaction.org.uk

'Working with other groups presents its own challenges, but it is very rewarding to be able to stand back with others and say, "Look what we've achieved, let's try to do more."'

85. The MILE Project Advice Centre

According to a local survey in 1997, 30 per cent of respondents said they would make use of an advice centre if it was set up locally. A satellite Citizens Advice Centre was therefore set up at Maybridge Community Church in January 1999. It operates every Friday morning, from 10.00 a.m. – 1.00 p.m., to offer free and confidential advice from a trained CAB advisor.

HOW IT WORKS

The need for such an advice service in the area is affirmed in that the usage at any given session is comparable to that in the main bureau in the town centre. The aim is simply to provide a weekly advice centre that is within easy reach of local residents. The project provides an accessible, welcoming, child-friendly environment, offering refreshments in a pleasant waiting area. A strong partnership has been established between the MILE Project and the Citizens Advice Bureau.

DEVELOPMENT

It is hoped that the service offered by the Citizens Advice Centre can be extended, operating more regularly. The Centre is also planning to train workers to offer other specialist advice services such as counselling and pregnancy advice.

THINGS TO CONSIDER

- Would your Citizens Advice Bureau be interested in launching a similar partnership scheme in your community?
- Do you have a trained Citizens Advice Bureau counsellor in your church or could someone train in this role?
- How would you ensure the service you provide is welcoming and accessible?

HOW TO GET FUNDING

The Citizens Advice Bureau provides resources and trained advisers; Maybridge Community Church provides volunteers, refreshments and the premises used.

FOR ADVICE AND MORE INFORMATION CONTACT:

The MILE Project,
c/o Maybridge Community Church,
The Strand,
Maybridge,
Worthing,
West Sussex,
BN12 6DL
Tel: 01903 603337
Email: info@mile-project.org.uk
Web: www.mile-project.org.uk

'One of the most satisfying things about this service is that many clients call back to let us know what has happened. Many clients have said how good it is to have a local service. I feel that it encourages them to seek advice at an early stage, instead of waiting until the situation has reached crisis point.'

86. Avencare – Drop-In Service

The Avencare project in Preston, Lancashire, provides social support within the area while at the same time building and developing a sense of community. Avencare was originally initiated in 1997 by Catholic Caring Services as part of their community development programme. The project is now jointly run by a local Roman Catholic church and an Anglican church.

HOW IT WORKS

The Avencare Drop-in Service in the church centre is an opportunity for residents to meet with others in a social setting. Facilities offered include access to games, a pool table, a computer room, a TV and video room, daily newspapers and magazines as well as free tea, coffee and food. The drop-in also provides information and advice. Day trips have been organised for local people to places of interest and recreation. Part of the ethos of the project is to recruit and train local volunteers. This provides both a community resource and work experience for those involved. Many volunteers come from the local churches.

DEVELOPMENT

Future plans for the development of the Drop-in Service include the provision of new services such as chiropody, a community nurse, tenants support workers, benefits advice, alcohol and drug support and health information.

THINGS TO CONSIDER

- Does your church have the facilities to open a drop-in centre?

- If not, where might you obtain suitable premises? Where would the ideal location of your centre be?
- How might you staff a centre?
- What services would you provide?

HOW TO GET FUNDING

Avencare receives funding from a number of charitable trusts, including the Church Urban Fund, which has given start-up grants for three years.

FOR ADVICE AND MORE INFORMATION CONTACT:

Joseph Cobb,
Avencare,
c/o The Foxton Centre,
Knowsley Street,
Preston,
Lancashire
PR1 3SA
Tel/Fax: 01772 558404

'Avencare aims to develop initiatives that respond to the social needs of individuals, groups and families living in or frequenting Avenham and the surrounding area that may be experiencing difficulty.'

87. Nether Hall Community Life Centre

Doncaster Pentecostal Church was cut off from the people it wanted to reach. The area in which its building was situated had slowly been transformed from a residential into a commercial area. The church wanted to take a more active role in the community and so in 1998 it bought new premises and Nether Hall Community Life Centre was born.

HOW IT WORKS

Staffed by 44 volunteers (90 per cent from the church congregation) the NHCLC offers a wide range of services to the community. These include a coffee shop/café, clothes shop, lunch club, toddlers group, children's work, youth clubs and language classes. However, it doesn't stop there. NHCLC is committed to serving the whole community and so operates a street work programme, befriending and supporting homeless people and prostitutes in the area. The centre also offers a drug dependency service, which aims to assist people as they break free of their addictions.

DEVELOPMENT

Since it started, Nether Hall Community Life Centre has grown at an incredible rate. It now needs to extend its building to allow its work to continue to grow. The old church building has been sold to help finance this new development.

THINGS TO CONSIDER

- How could your church use its buildings to integrate itself further into the local community?
- Is your church building in the best location to serve local people?

- What are the needs of the people in your community?
- In what ways could your church start to meet those needs?

HOW TO GET FUNDING

Nether Hall Community Life Centre has received funding from the Single Regeneration Budget, charitable trusts and support from individuals. Grants from charitable trusts fund the salary of a youth worker and a drug dependency worker.

FOR ADVICE AND MORE INFORMATION CONTACT:

Grayson Jones,
Nether Hall Community Life Centre,
30 Nether Hall Road,
Doncaster,
DN1 2PW
Tel: 01302 366522
Fax: 01302 365785
Email: info@internationalcitychurch.com
Web: www.internationalcitychurch.com

'A church in the heart of the community, with the community at its heart.'

SECTION 11:

Hackney Marsh Partnership & Bromley by Bow Centre

88. Hackney Marsh Partnership – Kingsmead Kabin

The Kingsmead Estate, Hackney, was for decades one of the most notorious housing estates in the UK. Poverty, crime and drug abuse were rife, and steel shutters and security gates were common. It was this which first inspired two local church leaders, team rector Pete Hobson and the Revd Phil Stone, to set up the Kingsmead Kabin.

HOW IT WORKS

The Kabin operated a range of projects including IT facilities, advice rooms, help for the unemployed, a drop-in centre and a legal service in partnership with a local solicitor. But in 1997 the Hackney Marsh Partnership was set up by a group of local churches to build on the work already being done and take it to the next stage. It now operates a number of highly successful projects which are transforming the community – but what makes them so successful is their connected nature. For instance, clients of a parent and toddler group can instantly be referred to a credit union to help with financial difficulties. The HMP offers truly joined up solutions to the complicated problems of life. The Kabin is still an integral part of the work of the HMP.

DEVELOPMENT

A new IT facility is planned as a result of UK Online funding.

THINGS TO CONSIDER

- Could your church team up with others in the area to offer a more holistic and integrated approach to community work in your area?

- How might you provide a more connected service?
- Above all, the HMP values and empowers people. How might your church do this?

HOW TO GET FUNDING

The Hackney Marsh Partnership has received funding from a number of sources. The Church Urban Fund has been a major and faithful contributor over the years. Government funding has been received from the Neighbourhood Renewal and the Single Regeneration Budgets among others. The National Lottery Community Fund has also been a significant income source.

FOR ADVICE AND MORE INFORMATION CONTACT:

Andy Turner,
Hackney Marsh Partnership,
8–9 Kingsmead Way,
London,
E9 5QG
Tel: 020 8533 0882
Email: Info@kabin.fsnet.co.uk

'The Kabin is the heart of this community; they are such good people and they are really interested in us. For years this place was a tip, a dumping ground, but now it's getting better . . . we have got hope for the future.'

89. Hackney Marsh Partnership – Kingsmead Advice Service

Launched as a Kingsmead Kabin initiative in 1996, the Kingsmead Advice Service was established to help the residents of the estate. The service originally employed a part-time advice worker and was always oversubscribed. In 1999, funding was obtained to enable a more sustainable service to be offered.

HOW IT WORKS

The Kingsmead Advice Service offers free, good quality, confidential legal and general advice to its clients. The service assists the residents of the estate (and increasingly people from further afield) with the often complicated matters of debt, benefits and housing. Clients are given assistance filling in forms and advised as to the benefits to which they are entitled. In 2001, the service generated an income to the area of £200,000 – made up of debts written off and benefits received. More importantly though, the service has been instrumental in giving people control over fundamental areas of their lives, granting increased financial freedom to its clients.

DEVELOPMENT

To continue to grow and meet wider need, the Kingsmead Advice Service is planning to move beyond the Kingsmead estate. To this end, it is developing a number of outreach posts on other local estates.

THINGS TO CONSIDER

- How might your church work with local people to improve their financial situation?

- A project like this requires specialist knowledge and training. Does your church have a solicitor who could help you with this?

HOW TO GET FUNDING

Initially the Kingsmead Advice Service was given funding by City Parochial. However, its expansion and continued work has been made possible by funding from the National Lottery Community Fund.

FOR ADVICE AND MORE INFORMATION CONTACT:

Andy Turner,
Hackney Marsh Partnership,
8–9 Kingsmead Way,
London,
E9 5QG
Tel: 020 8533 0882
Email: Info@kabin.fsnet.co.uk

'Two things can make a difference to places like Kingsmead and the surrounding area – money and Christ. The Kingsmead Advice Service offers both of these.'

90. Hackney Marsh Partnership – Kidstuff

Established by Kingsmead Kabin in 1995, Kidstuff is a simple project which provides quality goods for children at a minimal cost. Working on the Kingsmead Estate, Kidstuff not only helps parents to buy the things that their children need, but also converts the profits into subsidised days out.

HOW IT WORKS

The Kidstuff project is staffed by eight volunteers who undertake all of the work. Clothes, toys and other children's goods are gathered from a variety of sources, including church donations, shops (mainly end-of-line or shop-soiled items) and manufacturers. These goods are then sorted and sold to the public each Tuesday, Wednesday and Friday. The profits from the sale are then recycled and put towards special family trips also organised by Kidstuff. Regular customers get a loyalty card to allow them to gain points and go on more trips. The scheme essentially aims to increase the quality of life of local families by turning the purchase of necessities into the provision of a luxury.

DEVELOPMENT

Ultimately it is hoped that Kidstuff might become an independent business, moving into a shop front. However, high property prices make this harder to achieve.

THINGS TO CONSIDER

- Kidstuff is a great idea that could be emulated anywhere in the country as all it requires is a few volunteers, a building for the sales and a lot of enthusiasm. Could your church rise to the challenge?

- From what sources might you gather goods to sell?
- What kinds of trips might you organise in your area?

HOW TO GET FUNDING

Kidstuff has received some funding from the Children's Fund. However its running costs are minimal and it is working towards financial independence. In 2001 the project made £8,000, all of which was ploughed back into the community.

FOR ADVICE AND MORE INFORMATION CONTACT:

Andy Turner,
Hackney Marsh Partnership,
8–9 Kingsmead Way,
London,
E9 5QG
Tel: 020 8533 0882
Email: Info@kabin.fsnet.co.uk

'Let the little children come to me, and do not hinder them, for the kingdom of God belongs to such as these. I tell you the truth, anyone who will not receive the kingdom of God like a little child will never enter it.' (Mark 10:14f.)

91. Hackney Marsh Partnership – Stepping Up

In 1998, the HMP established an education, training and employment project which has evolved into Stepping Up, an initiative which promotes lifelong learning and attempts to enable people to identify and realise their life ambitions through education. Stepping Up provides information, support and advice on how to access training and employment opportunities.

HOW IT WORKS

Stepping Up aims simply to give people the boost that they need to realise their goals and their potential. A staff of six full-time workers (along with several specialised teams of volunteers) operates projects in a number of settings. A team which focuses on the needs of young people runs a mentoring programme in several local schools working with both primary and secondary pupils. A youth offending team deals with youngsters who have had brushes with the law. Added to these schemes is an initiative that works in local nightclubs. All of these projects fulfil the goals of Stepping Up: to increase people's self-esteem, to give them new confidence and to build in them an understanding of their personal value.

DEVELOPMENT

Stepping Up is developing a university programme to allow local residents to access higher education.

THINGS TO CONSIDER

- How could your church help in the motivation and education of local people?

- How might you foster a sense of self-worth in the people you have dealings with?
- What practical measures can you offer to help people find the right employment or education opportunities in your area?

HOW TO GET FUNDING

Although it receives no funding from the local council, Stepping Up has been funded by the government Single Regeneration and Neighbourhood Renewal Budgets, among others. Another significant source of funding has been the Church Urban Fund.

FOR ADVICE AND MORE INFORMATION CONTACT:

Andy Turner,
Hackney Marsh Partnership,
8–9 Kingsmead Way,
London,
E9 5QG
Tel: 020 8533 0882
Email: Info@kabin.fsnet.co.uk

'I feel much more confident now. I used to think I'd never achieve anything and that I'd be here for the rest of my life . . . now I know that I can do anything I want; I have the power to make my own choices.'

92. The Bromley by Bow Centre

The Bromley by Bow Centre has come a long way in 18 years. Back in 1984 the site on which the centre's plush set of buildings stand was occupied by an old church building (with 12 people and £400 in the bank) and a derelict park. Now the site boasts a dynamic community facility which has to be seen to be believed.

HOW IT WORKS

Tower Hamlets, the borough in which the centre is situated, is one of the most deprived areas of the UK, facing huge problems of unemployment, crime and poverty. However, the ethos of BBBC is to translate problems into opportunities. It views the projects it runs as being owned not by itself but by the community. It operates over 100 projects, many of which feed into each other, building a complex web of activities. The overarching goal is valuing people – to this end all of the facilities offered by the centre are of unsurpassed quality.

DEVELOPMENT

As it lives out its motto of putting 'people before structures', the Bromley by Bow Centre is constantly seeking new ways to help the people who use it and to encourage others in.

THINGS TO CONSIDER

- How can you transform your church building into a site which welcomes all of the people in your community?
- What facilities do you have and how might they be used to serve the community?
- Every journey starts with a single step – what is that step for your church?

HOW TO GET FUNDING

The Bromley by Bow Centre has received funding from a wide variety of sources. Some of its projects generate income. Significant funding has come from statutory grants such as the Single Regeneration Budget. Further to this is corporate sponsorship, charitable trust grants and, to a limited degree, one-off gifts from individuals.

FOR ADVICE AND MORE INFORMATION CONTACT:

Rob Trimble,
Chief Executive Officer,
The Bromley by Bow Centre,
St Leonard's Street,
Bromley by Bow,
London,
E3 3BT
Tel: 020 8709 9700
Fax: 020 8880 6608
Email: connect@bbbc.org.uk
Web: www.bbbc.org.uk

'With over 100 different activities, and in excess of 2,000 users every week, the Bromley by Bow Centre is a busy place, full of life and energy and determination to build a better community.'

93. BBBC – Healthy Living Centre

One of the most significant services offered by the Bromley by Bow Centre is its healthcare provision. The main building of the centre houses the majority of the projects, with a central reception desk which serves all of the facilities including a doctors' surgery. The centre's radical approach focuses on health rather than on illness.

HOW IT WORKS

The Healthy Living Centre recognises that many people visit their GP not because they are suffering from any medical condition, but rather because they are lonely and isolated, which makes them depressed and in desperate need of social interaction and a sense of belonging. Added to this, many patients suffer from ill health because of their unhealthy lifestyles. These issues represent a significant drain on the time of GPs and the resources of the NHS.

DEVELOPMENT

BBBC integrates traditional healthcare within the context of the community facilities they can offer. For example, someone who is suffering from depression can be given medical treatment as well as a chance to explore and express their interests (perhaps in a pottery or woodwork class) which inevitably restores their feeling of self-worth and their zest for life. This simple step of treating the person rather than the illness has proved so successful that Healthy Living Centres are being adopted across the UK.

THINGS TO CONSIDER

- Could your church offer healthcare facilities?
- If you don't feel that you could consider offering a full GPs' surgery, could you work in partnership with local medical practitioners to provide more holistic treatment?
- Even if you don't feel that healthcare is something your church can provide, what can you learn from the BBBC model?

HOW TO GET FUNDING

The BBBC Healthy Living Centre is funded in a variety of different ways, mostly by statutory funding from the NHS.

FOR ADVICE AND MORE INFORMATION CONTACT:

Rob Trimble,
Chief Executive Officer
The Bromley by Bow Centre,
St Leonard's Street,
Bromley by Bow,
London,
E3 3BT
Tel: 020 8709 9700
Fax: 020 8880 6608
Email: connect@bbbc.org.uk
Web: www.bbbc.org.uk

'We aim to explore and deliver new ways of improving the community's health, recognising the connection between the physical, the social and the spiritual.'

94. BBBC – Community Care

Functioning as part of the Healthy Living Centre, the Community Care programme of the Bromley by Bow Centre seeks to provide help to the many people in the community suffering from disabilities. The scheme offers care to those who need it while remaining faithful to two of BBBC's golden rules – 'value the individual' and 'problems equal opportunities'.

HOW IT WORKS

Two problems were observed in Bromley by Bow: first a rising number of people with disabilities who had been failed by statutory care by being given over to 'care in the community' in a community which did not seem to care. Second, a large number of young women who were largely housebound during the day, doing nothing but watching daytime TV and growing increasingly excluded from society. BBBC's Community Care programme brought these two groups together, enabling the disabled people to get the care they needed and the women to be reintegrated into community. The women involved in the project value the disabled people whom they serve, and in so doing find themselves valued.

DEVELOPMENT

The Community Care programme has fed into other areas of the work of BBBC – many of its volunteers now work in different initiatives run by the centre.

THINGS TO CONSIDER

- What facilities are available for disabled people in your area?
- How might your church be instrumental in helping isolated and socially excluded people in your community?

- In what other ways could your church develop synergies between different people groups with which it works?

HOW TO GET FUNDING

BBBC Community Care receives funding from a wide variety of sources, including the Single Regeneration Budget and many of the funds set aside for deprived areas.

FOR ADVICE AND MORE INFORMATION CONTACT:

Rob Trimble,
Chief Executive Officer,
The Bromley by Bow Centre,
St Leonard's Street,
Bromley by Bow,
London,
E3 3BT
Tel: 020 8709 9700
Fax: 020 8880 6608
Email: connect@bbbc.org.uk
Web: www.bbbc.org.uk

'We aim to engage the local community in identifying issues of concern relating to the social and physical environment that affects people's everyday lives.'

95. BBBC – Child Care

One of the first services offered by the Bromley by Bow Centre was child care. In an area that had limited facilities for the care of children, a service was needed to enable parents to work or simply to have some time for themselves. The child care service of BBBC now works with 40 children each day.

HOW IT WORKS

The service grew from a nursery operated by a group of women within a local house. These women approached the church enquiring about the possibility of using the church facilities. The nursery runs in the original church building to this day, a building which has been remodelled to provide the most versatile space for many groups. An important principle of the BBBC model is that of 'mixed economy'. This means that the children who use the facility come from a wide range of social and ethnic backgrounds – some the children of professionals, some children identified as at risk. This principle produces quality both in terms of the service provided as well as the social environment of the nursery.

DEVELOPMENT

Plans are afoot to establish another child care facility nearby to allow care to be offered to a greater number of children.

THINGS TO CONSIDER

- What other child care facilities are available in your area?
- Could your church offer child care which surpasses the quality of existing facilities?
- How might you attract children from a wide spectrum of backgrounds?

- How would you need to develop your existing church facilities in order to set up a child care project?

HOW TO GET FUNDING

The BBBC Child care programme receives much of its funding from daily fees paid by parents (either at a full or subsidised rate, depending on their circumstances). Further income is generated through statutory funding, especially through the Single Regeneration Budget and Neighbourhood Nursery Initiative.

FOR ADVICE AND MORE INFORMATION CONTACT:

Rob Trimble,
Chief Executive Officer,
The Bromley by Bow Centre,
St Leonard's Street,
Bromley by Bow,
London,
E3 3BT
Tel: 020 8709 9700
Fax: 020 8880 6608
Email: connect@bbbc.org.uk
Web: www.bbbc.org.uk

'The Bromley by Bow Centre is a pioneering voluntary organisation that has transformed its local community. It continues to do so in new and innovative ways.'

96. BBBC – Pie in the Sky Café

Everything at the Bromley by Bow Centre is of exceptional quality and this is nowhere more obvious than in the 'Pie in the Sky café'. Looking more like a West End Italian restaurant than an East End voluntary sector establishment, the café serves food as the centre serves the community.

HOW IT WORKS

It would be wrong to suggest that 'Pie in the Sky' is just a place to eat – it is so much more than that. It functions as an art gallery displaying original works from some of the artists who are integral to all that BBBC does. It is a training kitchen offering people a chance to learn culinary skills in a professional environment. It is also an incubator for local enterprise, its facilities being used by people who are setting up catering businesses in the area. A local woman has started such a venture with the help of the café, and two young men have started a pizza business which is open on a couple of nights each week.

DEVELOPMENT

BBBC is constantly looking for new enterprises to support, empowering local people to make a difference to their own lives.

THINGS TO CONSIDER

- Could your church open a community café?
- What facilities would you need and how would you obtain them?
- How could your café be used to support local people?
- How would you go about providing the best quality service?

HOW TO GET FUNDING

The Pie in the Sky café generates much of its own funding, operating as a successful business.

FOR ADVICE AND MORE INFORMATION CONTACT:

Rob Trimble,
Chief Executive Officer,
The Bromley by Bow Centre,
St Leonard's Street,
Bromley by Bow,
London,
E3 3BT
Tel: 020 8709 9700
Fax: 020 8880 6608
Email: connect@bbbc.org.uk
Web: www.bbbc.org.uk

'We strive for excellence in all that we build and all that we provide. We believe that integrated services meet the diverse needs of our community. We are passionate about partnerships that make the most of available resources.'

97. BBBC – Enterprises

Back in the days when the Bromley by Bow Centre was a struggling church, a group of local artists began to use its facilities as studio space. Rather than paying rent in money, they offered their skills and artwork as payment. The centre now offers support to a host of local enterprises in the same way.

HOW IT WORKS

Art is still a major focus of the centre, with all of the many pieces on display around the buildings produced on site. Studio space is provided for stained-glass window making, stone-carving, woodwork, silkscreen printing, textiles, etc. Local people can use the facilities to establish their own enterprises – people come in, learn skills and then turn their newfound abilities to profit by selling what they have made. A fully equipped enterprise room is available to help people research and develop their plans. The centre sees itself as an incubator for these ventures, recognising that some may stay while others may become self-sufficient and independent businesses. In total there are 43 enterprises run from the centre, ranging from the manufacture of furniture to hairdressing.

DEVELOPMENT

The centre is keen to develop the ideas of local people and is always on the lookout for new enterprises.

THINGS TO CONSIDER

- How could your church be involved in helping local people get a business off the ground?
- How could your church facilities be used to empower people in this way?

- Any group of people have a range of skills. What skills are present in your church and how could you teach these to others?

HOW TO GET FUNDING

BBBC Enterprises are funded largely by statutory funds, including the Single Regeneration Budget. Many of the enterprises are funded at least in part by their own activities.

FOR ADVICE AND MORE INFORMATION CONTACT:

Rob Trimble,
Chief Executive Officer,
The Bromley by Bow Centre,
St Leonard's Street,
Bromley by Bow,
London,
E3 3BT
Tel: 020 8709 9700
Fax: 020 8880 6608
Email: connect@bbbc.org.uk
Web: www.bbbc.org.uk

'We aim to use art as a vehicle for breaking down the boundaries between the environment, health, enterprise and education – unlocking the creative potential of individuals, recognising the possibilities within all of us.'

98. BBBC – Communiversity

Education is an important part of the work carried out by the Bromley by Bow Centre. As in many deprived wards, a trend of young people leaving school without any formal qualifications was observed. This problem fed into the wider issue of unemployment in the area. The BBBC started its education programmes in response to this need.

HOW IT WORKS

Most people would identify kids who leave education without qualifications as people who failed at school; BBBC instead recognises that many of these young people were failed *by* school. The centre offers various education programmes which lead to recognised qualifications. BBBC runs such courses as Teaching English as a Second Language (TEASL) and Child care, which leads to an NVQ. HNC and HND qualifications (awarded by Middlesex University) are also available. The programme has around 80 graduates, most of whom left school with no qualifications.

DEVELOPMENT

The future of the education programmes at BBBC is exciting. The centre is currently developing the 'Communiversity', a scheme which will offer education to university level within the centre. Clearly such a scheme will have a massive impact on the community as it allows local people to access a whole new range of employment opportunities.

THINGS TO CONSIDER

- How could your church serve those people who have been failed by the education system?

- What skills could your church teach?
- How might you work in partnership with existing education programmes?

HOW TO GET FUNDING

The BBBC Communiversity receives funds from a range of sources. Its education programmes attract statutory funding.

FOR ADVICE AND MORE INFORMATION CONTACT:

Rob Trimble,
Chief Executive Officer,
The Bromley by Bow Centre,
St Leonard's Street,
Bromley by Bow,
London,
E3 3BT
Tel: 020 8709 9700
Fax: 020 8880 6608
Email: connect@bbbc.org.uk
Web: www.bbbc.org.uk

'Our activities and environment promote an expectation of success, challenge low self-esteem and raise aspirations. We refuse to accept mediocrity.'

SECTION 12:

Town Planning

99. Churches Together in Ashford

Ashford in Kent is one of the fastest growing towns in Europe. Plans are currently being drawn up to increase this development with up to 1,900 new homes being built every year for the next 30 years. The Revd Simon Ellis, employed by Ashford's churches, is involved in working with the local council in the planning of the town's growth.

HOW IT WORKS

Simon's primary role is working with the planning of new developments. His involvement in the process of town planning ensures that the church is not forgotten or sidelined, but rather is considered as a valuable partner. He has found that the church needs to be united in order to be heard, and his role as the voice of the churches in Ashford has allowed efficient communication between them, local government and other agencies. Simon has become heavily involved in all areas of the development process, including the allocation of funding, chairing the local Children's Fund partnership, sitting on the Sure Start Board, as well as being a member of the Local Strategic Partnership and involved in the Area Investment Framework.

DEVELOPMENT

Through Simon, Churches Together in Ashford remains on the cutting edge of town planning as Ashford faces the changes of the coming years. This gives them a key role in thinking about such facilities as new schools, healthcare and leisure amenities, as well as the positioning of church buildings.

THINGS TO CONSIDER

- How is it planned that your town will develop in the future?
- What steps could your church take to engage with the council's plans?
- Could you work in partnership with the other churches in your area to speak with a united voice?
- How might you find funds to employ someone like Simon to represent all of the local churches?

HOW TO GET FUNDING

Simon's role is funded by a local partnership, which provides his salary (Diocese of Canterbury), house (United Reformed Church) and other costs (Baptist and Methodist churches) with local churches covering expenses. A final partner is Ashford Borough Council, which provides office space and significant support for the project.

FOR ADVICE AND MORE INFORMATION CONTACT:

The Revd Simon Ellis,
c/o Community Services,
Ashford Borough Council,
Tannery Lane,
Ashford,
Kent,
TN23 1PL
Email: simon.ellis@ashford.gov.uk

'Some people say "You seem to pop up everywhere!" But it's just that when you really want to be involved, there are always ways in which you can be.'

100. Purley Baptist Church – Community Redevelopment

Purley Baptist Church has been considering redeveloping its present buildings for many years. However, it was realised that a wider vision was called for, not only in terms of their future location, but also in relation to its involvement and position within the community of Purley. The church is now involved with the redevelopment of the whole of Purley town centre.

HOW IT WORKS

Purley Baptist Church has identified an opportunity to impact its community on a massive scale. Not only do the plans include the purchase of several new buildings in a strategic location but also a partnership with Croydon Council. PBC has won a seat at the 'top table' concerning the redevelopment of the town. In partnership with the council, the church aims to redevelop a specific area of the town – a large triangular 'island' near the town centre. This new development will include a traffic scheme to improve flow, new church buildings, a café/restaurant and meditation garden, health and sports facilities, and much more.

DEVELOPMENT

The project is still very much in the planning stages, but when the work is complete it will provide significant ongoing benefits for the whole town and all the people of Purley.

THINGS TO CONSIDER

- What are your local council's future plans for the development of your area?
- Can you see a way in which your church could be involved

in the formulation and development of these plans?
- How radical are you willing to be?

HOW TO GET FUNDING

As the project develops, funding will become available from various local, regional and central government pots. However, Purley Baptist Church has also committed huge resources to the project – especially in the purchase of several derelict shops.

FOR ADVICE AND MORE INFORMATION CONTACT:

Mike Fixter MRICS – Head of Facilities,
Purley Baptist Church,
Banstead Road,
Purley,
Surrey,
CR8 3EA
Tel: 020 8668 0422
Fax: 020 8660 6742
Web: www.purleybaptist.org
Email: office@purleybaptist.org

'Purley Baptist Church wants to be at the hub of its community, physically as well as spiritually – offering it holistic and readily accessible services.'

How to Get Involved

The Faithworks movement exists:

- to empower and inspire individual Christians and every local church to develop its role at the hub of its community;
- to challenge and change the public perception of the church by engaging with both media and government;
- to promote Christian values within our society.

In this book we have looked at 100 different projects which are truly transforming communities. People cannot but be changed when they meet the God of love. We believe that it is better to demonstrate God than simply to talk about him – because in demonstrating his love we are not asking people to believe what we are saying; we are asking them to receive what he is doing.

Faithworks is all about helping local churches to engage more effectively with the business of Christianity – loving God and loving people. Hopefully this book will have given you some ideas of how you might either make a start or take another step. The good news is that you don't have to struggle on alone; there are people to help you and ways that you can be supported. As well as all of the contributors to this book who have provided contact details for you to get in touch to seek advice, you can also get guidance and support from Faithworks and the Faithworks Partners.

If we are going to work in our communities and in partnership with other agencies and local and national government, then we need to be committed to do so in a professional manner. As part of your commitment to ongoing professionalism why not sign the Faithworks Charter? Put together by a team of professionals, including practitioners, church leaders, lawyers and policy makers, the Faithworks Charter is a 'benchmark' for local churches, Christian agencies and projects to sign up to and then work hard towards. A growing number of churches and Christian agencies are adopting it. But more than that, a number of local councils now regard it as their 'standard' when considering partnership with local Christian projects.

THE FAITHWORKS CHARTER

PRINCIPLES FOR CHURCHES AND LOCAL CHRISTIAN AGENCIES COMMITTED TO EXCELLENCE IN COMMUNITY WORK AND SERVICE PROVISION IN THE UK.

Motivated by our Christian faith we commit ourselves to serve others by assuring the following standards in all our community work within 12 months of signing this charter.

Service to the community

1. To serve and to respect all people regardless of their gender, marital status, race, ethnic origin, religion, age, sexual orientation or physical and mental capability.
2. To acknowledge the freedom of people of all faiths or none both to hold and to express their beliefs and convictions respectfully and freely, within the limits of the UK law.
3. Never to impose our Christian faith or belief on others.
4. To develop partnerships with other churches, voluntary groups, statutory agencies and local government wherever appropriate in order to create an effective, integrated service for our clients avoiding unnecessary duplication of resources.
5. To provide and to publicise regular consultation and

reporting forums to client groups and the wider community regarding the effective development and delivery of our work and our responsiveness to their actual needs.

Clients, staff and volunteers

1. To create an environment where clients, volunteers and employees are encouraged and enabled to realise their potential.
2. To assist our clients, volunteers and employees to take responsibility for their own learning and development, both through formal and informal training opportunities and ongoing assessment.
3. To develop an organisational culture in which individuals learn from any mistakes made and where excellence and innovation are encouraged and rewarded.
4. To promote the value of a balanced, holistic lifestyle as part of each individual's overall personal development.
5. To abide by the requirements of employment law in the UK and to implement best employment practices and procedures whilst ensuring that our clients are served by those who share and respect our distinctive ethos and values.

Management and outcomes

1. To implement a management structure that fosters and encourages participation by staff at all levels in order to facilitate the fulfilment of the project's goals and visions.
2. To set and to review measurable and timed outcomes annually, and regularly to evaluate and monitor our management structure and output, recognising the need for ongoing organisational flexibility, development and good stewardship of resources.
3. To do all we can to ensure that we are not over-dependent on any one source of funding.
4. To implement best practice procedures in terms of Health and Safety and Child Protection in order to protect our staff, volunteers and clients.

5. To handle our funding in a transparent and accountable way and to give relevant people from outside our organisation/project reasonable access to our accounts.

To sign the Faithworks Charter on behalf of your church or project, write to obtain a copy from :
Faithworks,
115 Southwark Bridge Road,
London,
SE1 0AX
or visit www.faithworks.info

THE FAITHWORKS CONSULTANCY

The Faithworks Consultancy exists to empower and inspire every local church to rediscover its role at the heart of community by providing the following:

Nationwide expertise to help turn your local vision into reality

Our national team of practitioners are ready to serve you by sharing their experience and expertise at every stage as you seek to turn your vision for community engagement into reality. Practical advice and assistance is offered in all areas of community development, including education, finance, strategic planning, management, health, housing, children's work, youth work, government and social work.

As a church you may be just starting to consider effective community engagement and need a mentor to help you through the process of auditing your community. Or you may have been running a highly successful community programme for a number of years and now require specialist advice on planning for the future. Whatever position your church finds itself in, Faithworks is committed to matching our resources with your needs as you seek to serve your community more effectively.

Training options to help you to begin thinking through the issues

We can provide seminars to help your local church or churches begin to unpack issues of social justice, project identification, strategic planning, partnership with local government, etc.

Day Training Seminars for churches and projects

For churches who want to work with local government, but don't know where to start, these day seminars will equip you to make the most of the opportunities partnership can offer.

Contact the Faithworks Consultancy if you want more help on any of the following:

- How to turn your vision into reality
- How to accurately assess your community's needs
- How to identify and develop your church's resources
- How to develop a credible strategic/business plan
- How to build strategic partnerships with local government and other agencies
- How to access funding sources.

Contact Faithworks Consultancy now:

Faithworks Consultancy,
115 Southwark Bridge Road,
London,
SE1 0AX
Tel: 020 7450 9086
Email: Tim Waldron at consultancy@faithworks.info

BECOMING A FAITHWORKS MEMBER

In order to make a real impact on government and media, we have to learn to stand and speak together with one voice. Now is the time to address the government's agenda and to work with it to explore practical ways in which the church can play its full role in rebuilding the safety net of community care around the UK. Now is the time to say loud and clear that we believe faith works, to tackle the negative media coverage of the church and tell the story once again of Christ transforming lives and communities.

The Faithworks movement exists to tell your story and give you a voice that can be heard in government as well as equip you in service to your local community and enable you to work together with tens of thousands of others across the UK to demonstrate that faith works.

Alone we will never be heard. But together we can make a difference. In becoming a member of the Faithworks movement you will be declaring with one voice that faith works! You will be helping to create a mandate for change, as we endeavour to engage on your behalf with both government and media at a national level. As a member you will also benefit from access to a huge range of Faithworks services, tools and resources. Free membership is available to individuals, churches and faith-based community projects.

To register as a member of the Faithworks movement, whether as an individual, a church or a faith-based community project, visit www.faithworks.info, call 020 7490 9052, or write to:

Faithworks Membership,
115 Southwark Bridge Road,
London,
SE1 OAX

The Faithworks Partners

The Faithworks movement is built around eleven leading Christian organisations that have committed to work together to provide expertise, tools and resources to churches as they seek to engage with their local community. The following pages give further information on their ministries.

CARE

CARE aims to serve, inform and equip you, offering people, ideas, information and resources to churches and individuals who are seeking to be 'salt and light' in their communities.

CARE is a charity that runs projects across the UK, making a tangible Christian difference through networks of volunteers. It is active in public life and undertakes practical caring initiatives that affect the lives of thousands.

CARE aims to help you be part of the answer.

Caring

- A hospitality network provides hospitality and refuge, with 350 Christian homes across the UK and a counselling referral service.
- Pregnancy crisis – CARE offers support, advice, information on all options and ongoing practical support, with 150 UK centres.
- Radical care – provides 'forever families', foster care for young people on remand and befriending of adults with learning disabilities.

Campaigning

- CARE campaigns across the UK, in Brussels and the UN on issues of human dignity in family, health, education, politics and media.
- Community involvement – CARE provides training and

resourcing for Christians to be more effective light and salt, including over 500 school governors and hundreds participating in grassroots politics.

Communicating

- Getting the word out – CARE helps the church to be informed, active and effective with a Christian worldview and publishes specialist research to inform public debate.
- The next generation – CARE is involved in shaping education policy, getting resources into thousands of schools, speaking to youth about relationships, and facilitating prayer networks for 2,000 schools.

National helplines:

CARELINK – 08457 626 536
linking you to the care you need via a database of 3,000 specialist agencies in 60 categories

CARELINE – 0800 028 2228
providing free, confidential access to advice and counselling on pregnancy and post-abortion care

CHILDLINK – 0845 601 1134
helping those helping children with comprehensive information on child care issues

CARE – London, Glasgow, Belfast, Cardiff, Brussels

Head office:
53 Romney Street,
London, SW1P 3RF
Tel: 08453 100 244
Email: mail@care.org.uk
Web: www.care.org.uk
Registered charity no: 1066963

CARE FOR THE FAMILY

Care for the Family's heart is to strengthen family life and to help those who are hurting because of family trauma.

It is their strong belief that prevention is better than cure and that's why they put so much effort into events and seminars for those with already good relationships – to provide quality input so that they can survive the hard times that usually do come along. Most of the programmes are specifically geared to be available to the whole community – not only the faith groups. They are often publicised by churches who see the value of such programmes to the whole of their community contacts. Previous titles include: The Sixty Minute Marriage, Beating Burnout, Maintaining a Healthy Marriage and The Heart of a Parent.

They also have a number of specific programmes that are delivered at a local community level by those in local churches. The Rapport workshops, Developing Closeness in Marriage and Resolving Everyday Issues, are presented to couples all over the country by trained leaders, often at the request of a 'sponsoring' fellowship. The new training department will provide materials and support for those who wish to run small groups addressing marriage and parenting issues in their local area on behalf of and for any community group with whom they are networked.

Opportunities for new activity are continually being offered and the next year will see an expansion of their work with single parents, step parents, those maturing in years and those parents who have experienced the bereavement of a child. In all these new initiatives, Care for the Family will be partnering with churches who can help bring support to their local community.

Care for the Family
Registered Office:
Garth House,
Leon Avenue,
Cardiff,
CF15 7RG
Tel: 029 2081 1733
Fax: 029 2081 4089
Web: care.for.the.family@ccf.org.uk

CARITAS SOCIAL ACTION

Caritas Social Action is an umbrella body for Catholic Charities in England and Wales. It seeks to support, empower and coordinate those involved in the reduction of poverty and social exclusion in England and Wales, and to ensure that the 'option for the poor' is incarnate in the life of the church. Caritas is also part of a wider European and international network of Catholic charities.

There are hundreds of Catholic charities in England and Wales with a combined annual turnover of over £50m involving approximately 500,000 staff and volunteers who meet the needs of thousands of individuals, families and communities of all faiths and none.

For more information, to donate or participate, please contact:

Caritas Social Action,
39 Eccleston Square,
London,
SWIV IBX
Tel: 020 7901 4875
Web: www.caritas-socialaction.org.uk

caritas
social action

CHRISTIAN HERALD

As the UK's only interdenominational Christian weekly newspaper, the heartbeat of *Christian Herald* is the local church. Every week, the paper is packed with news of grassroots activity that is making a difference – local churches finding needs to meet, thinking creatively about serving their local community and forging partnerships to improve life for those living around them.

Christian Herald is committed to equipping Christians in a number of ways:

- By helping readers understand the contemporary issues of the day from a biblical standpoint.
- By telling the stories of local churches that are making their presence felt, day by day, in their villages, towns and cities.
- By stretching readers' thinking – stressing that the gospel has something to say and something to do, no matter what the area of contemporary life.
- By providing the information and challenge that can help stir Christians into life wherever God has placed them: work, home, school, neighbourhood.

Russ Bravo, Editor of *Christian Herald*, says: 'It's our conviction that for a resurgent church to bring the life and love of Christ to a desperately lost world, it must begin to engage with it sacrificially, humbly and passionately. We hope to help in that process.'

Christian Media Centre Ltd,
96 Dominion Road,
Worthing,
West Sussex,
BN14 8JP
Tel: 01903 821082
Fax: 01903 821081
Web: www.christianherald.org.uk
Registered in England No. 2205345

Christian

CHRISTIANITY+RENEWAL

Christianity+Renewal is a monthly magazine with a readership of over 30,000 who are drawn to its lively mix of news, analysis, columnists, reviews and loads more. Regular contributors include Tony Campolo, Steve Chalke, Gerald Coates, Jane Collins, Margaret Ellis, Rob Frost, Mark Greene, Joyce Huggett, Jeff Lucas, Mike Pilavachi and Rob Warner.

Christianity+Renewal magazine was launched in 2001 – a merger of two popular and respected titles with their roots in the evangelical and charismatic parts of the church. This 70-plus page magazine aims to reflect its tag line: real life, real faith, in the real world. The readership is drawn from right across the denominations.

The magazine also carries news stories outlining the substantial improvements in communication between Faithworks and government bodies.

Another regular article, 'Living Churches', features local churches that are making a difference in their community. Articles identify ideas, principles, programmes and initiatives that other churches can learn from and adapt in their own situation.

Christianity+Renewal encompasses news, culture, reviews, persecuted church news, spirituality, biblical strategies, websites to visit, devotions, insight, leadership issues, theological reflection, true-life ministry stories, plus pages of jobs.

The magazine is available from all good Christian bookshops, price £2.50, or through your letterbox by subscription.

CREDIT ACTION

Credit Action is a national education charity, established in 1994. Before becoming an independent charity, it was part of the Jubilee Centre in Cambridge.

Through the media exposure and resources it produces, Credit Action wants to encourage the population at large to have confidence in handling their own money. Major companies, including Boots, Nat West Bank, Sun Life and the Body Shop, have used their materials in the past.

Individuals

Credit Action wants to ensure as many as possible avoid the pain of debt, by helping them to manage their money more effectively. They produce a range of self-help guides and other publications, aimed at encouraging sensible money management for those currently facing some form of debt, and provide video and study notes for group use in Christian fellowships, though individuals can also benefit from this resource.

Credit Action recognises that many people who contact them will already be in some sort of financial difficulty, so they have very close links with the major debt counselling charity, the Consumer Credit Counselling Service. The CCCS provides debt counselling and management services free of charge. Go to www.cccs.co.uk for more information.

Churches

Credit Action also serves local churches by providing a variety of training seminars on the biblical and practical principles of better money management, with the aim of helping both congregations and communities in this area.

They speak widely at conferences and other events, providing speakers for local churches when asked, and believe that money and debt advice can be an effective and useful service provided by local church groups and other community-based groups.

For further information please contact:

Keith Tondeur,
National Director,
Regent Terrace,
Cambridge,
CB2 1AA
Tel: 01223 324 034
Email: office@creditaction.com
Web: www.creditaction.com

MOORLANDS COLLEGE

Moorlands College provides a challenging learning environment where men and women, passionate about Jesus Christ, may be nurtured and equipped to impact both the church and the world.

As an evangelical, interdenominational Bible college, Moorlands aims for the highest standards in delivering courses that are biblically based, academically rigorous and culturally relevant, grounding everything in practice to facilitate effective service in today's world, and creating a supportive community which promotes spiritual, personal and relational maturity.

In the past decade or so Moorlands has recognised the crucial nature of understanding what is happening to culture and of building courses that equip students to engage relevantly in community work of all types in a professional and biblically coherent fashion.

The formally agreed Aims and Objectives for two of the most popular courses, Community and Family Studies and Youth and Community Work, resonate significantly with the Faithworks goals.

For many years Moorlands has educated and trained just a select number of students, who, when they graduate, have the learning, the experience and the skills to work with churches, Christian organisations and local authorities in community development work. Through partnership with Faithworks, Moorlands will now be in a position to share specialist course content and its expertise in training and mentoring with a much wider audience – helping local churches to mobilise their members towards effective community projects.

Moorlands College,
Sopley,
Christchurch,
Dorset,
BH23 7AT
Tel: 01425 672369
Fax: 01425 674162
Email: mail@moorlands.ac.uk

OASIS TRUST

Oasis Charitable Trust is an organisation committed to demonstrating the Christian faith in action. It works in communities across the world, seeking to provide holistic solutions to the major social issues of our time.

Oasis focuses its activities on the poor and marginalised in society and seeks to equip others to engage in similar work in order to increase the impact of the projects in which it gets involved.

Oasis was founded in 1985 by Steve Chalke. It is organised into four major areas of innovative activity:

- *Community Action* – working housing and healthcare in some of the most vulnerable urban areas, it seeks to teach life skills and to break the cycle of no home, no job.
- *Global Action* – working directly and with partners in over 20 countries around the world. Through the exchange of people, expertise and resources it seeks to enable churches and communities to empower some of the world's poorest and most marginalised people.
- *Youth Action* – investing in training tomorrow's church and community leaders. It also runs social inclusion projects across London, focusing on those at risk of being excluded from the education system.
- *Church Action* – equipping the church through personnel, training, consultancy and projects. It also develops new models of culturally appropriate expressions of church for the twenty-first century. Oasis Church Action created

Faithworks to enable and inspire every local church to rediscover its role at the hub of the community.

For more information about Oasis, please contact:

Steve Chalke,
Oasis Trust,
The Oasis Centre,
115 Southwark Bridge Road,
London,
SE1 0AX
Tel: 020 7450 9000
Fax: 020 7450 9001
Email: enquiries@oasistrust.org
Web: www.oasistrust.org

THE SHAFTESBURY HOUSING GROUP

The Shaftesbury Housing Group is a professional charitable Christian organisation established to meet housing and care needs. As at January 2002 the Group provided homes and/or care services to over 20,000 people, primarily in the South of England.

Shaftesbury Housing was established by the Shaftesbury Society in 1970 and is now a separate organisation. The Group's Parent Association and two of its subsidiaries are Registered Social Landlords, giving access to Housing Corporation funding. The Group has a financial turnover of £60 million and employs approximately 1,400 staff.

The Group has a wide range of experience in relation to housing and care. This includes major urban regeneration, covering commercial development and training opportunities within multicultural communities. Specific examples are the regeneration of 1,000 homes in Hackney and the provision of a community-based housing association for management and improvement of 1,500 homes in Oxfordshire.

The current constituents of the Group are:

- Shaftesbury Housing Association – Parent Association providing family homes and sheltered housing (for rent and leasehold).
- Ashley Homes – residential care and supported housing.
- Banbury Homes Housing Association (community-based association providing family homes, sheltered housing and some supported housing).

- Kingsmead Homes Ltd – local housing company engaged in urban regeneration, provision of family homes, training and workshop units.
- SOAS Homes Ltd – student housing in London.
- Shaftesbury Student Housing Ltd – student housing and key worker accommodation.
- Cooper Homes & Developments Ltd – development company.

For further information please contact:

Clive Bodley,
Commercial Director,
Shaftesbury Housing Group,
1 Mawle Court,
Banbury,
Oxon,
OX16 5BH
Tel: 01295 261669
Fax: 01295 265995
Email: cdb@shaftesburyhousing.org.uk

STEWARDSHIP SERVICES

Stewardship Services is a national Christian charity committed to raising the standard of legal and financial administration in churches and Christian organisations. It provides a range of practical services to help organisations get started as a charity and to meet a number of the ongoing needs and responsibilities that they will face. These include:

Charity formation

Stewardship Services has extensive experience of registering charities and understands the Charity Commission and how to present applications to avoid undue delays. It can set you up with a charitable trust or charitable company specially designed for a church-based charity serving the community.

Payroll administration

Payroll can be a big burden. The service takes care of the details, producing payslips, making payment to the employee's bank account and dealing with tax and National Insurance.

Employment Contract Pack

Specially designed for use by a Christian charity, the pack contains a model contract of employment, with a number of variations and helpful guidance notes.

Gift Aid administration

Outsource tax-effective giving to Stewardship Services and enjoy fast and frequent tax recovery and release from the pressure of meeting Inland Revenue requirements.

Accounts examination service

An independent examination of accounts is a legal requirement when income reaches £10,000 pa. Stewardship Services is a specialist in this field.

Service standards and charges

Stewardship Services aims to provide professional quality at reasonable cost. Contact them for details of charges and discounts to Faithworks members.

Stewardship Services,
P.O. Box 99,
Loughton,
Essex,
IG10 3QJ
Tel: 020 8502 5600
Fax: 020 8502 5333
Email: info@stewardshipservices.org
Web: www.stewardshipservices.org
Registered charity no: 234714

YMCA

YMCAs are Christian charities belonging to a national and worldwide movement. They aim to offer young people and their communities opportunities to develop in mind, body and spirit, and so fulfil their potential. Working with people at times of greatest need, they believe in:

- personal and social development – providing life and job skills training and opportunities for personal growth and challenge;
- nourishing relationships – providing parenting programmes and activities which support young people's transition to adulthood;
- strong communities – providing housing, community activities and sport, health, exercise and fitness programmes.

The YMCA aims to underpin all its work with Christian principles and work for a society where all may flourish. Over 160 YMCAs make up the YMCA movement in England. Each is led by local people for local communities, developing projects to meet identified needs. These local energies are supported by national expertise.

The YMCA, through its local presence, can offer churches and Christian agencies general advice and support based on practical experience in developing and delivering community work and service provision. The YMCA is interested in working in partnership with other organisations that share its ethos and its aims. It has developed standards of best practice for many areas of its work in relation to staff and volunteers, and is willing to discuss how these may be used elsewhere.

YMCA England,
640 Forest Road,
London,
E17 3DZ
Tel: 020 8520 5599
Fax: 020 8509 3190
Web: www.ymca.org.uk

Index

Numbers refer to Ideas not pages.